Money Rules 101

101

Master Your Money
Before it Masters You

A Guide for Parents and Teens

Patti J. Handy

Published by: Inspired Thinkers Publishing
Valencia, California

Copyright @ Patti J. Handy and Teens Cash Coach. 2009-2017

Teens Cash Coach is a trademark of Patti J. Handy. All rights reserved.
www.teenscashcoach.com
www.pattihandy.com

Publisher's Cataloging-In-Publication Data
(Prepared by The Donohue Group, Inc.)

Names: Handy, Patti J.
Title: Money rules 101 : master your money before it masters you : a guide for parents
    and teens / Patti J. Handy.
Description: Valencia, California : Inspired Thinkers Publishing, [2017]
Identifiers: LCCN 2017900726 | ISBN 978-0-9824656-4-6 | ISBN 0-9824656-4-5 |
    ISBN 978-0-9824656-5-3 (ebook) | ISBN 0-9824656-5-3 (ebook)
Subjects: LCSH: Teenagers--Finance, Personal--Handbooks, manuals, etc. | Young
    adults--Finance, Personal--Handbooks, manuals, etc. | Money--Handbooks,
    manuals, etc. | Consumer credit--Handbooks, manuals, etc. | Life skills--
    Handbooks, manuals, etc.
Classification: LCC HG179 .H36 2017 (print) | LCC HG179 (ebook) | DDC
    332.024--dc23

ISBN: 0-9824656-4-5
ISBN-13: 978-0-9824656-4-6
Library of Congress Control Number 2017900726

This book is designed to provide accurate and reliable information in regard to the
subject matter covered. It is sold with the understanding that the author and
publisher, through this book, is not engaged in legal, accounting, financial, or other
professional services. Laws and practices often vary from state to state, and if legal,
financial, or other expert assistance is required, the services of a professional should
be sought. The author and publisher specifically disclaim any liability that is incurred
from the use or application of the contents of this book. Examples used within this
book are hypothetical in nature and are used for illustrative purposes only. They do
not take into consideration the consequence of fees or taxes and not indicative of any
specific investment or investment strategy. Investments seeking higher rates of return
generally involve a higher degree of risk of principal.

For ordering information or special discounts for bulk purchases, please email
support@teenscashcoach.com.

Printed in the United States of America

To My Mom and Dad ~

I am deeply grateful for your endless sacrifices,
support and a lifetime of love ...
Thank you from the bottom of my heart. I love you!

Patti J. Handy

A special thanks to:

My sisters, Cheryl Cunningham and Michelle Bernstorff, who are a constant source of support and love. My son, my inspiration and my *why*, Blake Gonzalez.
Judith Cassis, Circe Denyer, Jane Sanford,
Ricki Steigerwald and Terri Keefer Photography, all of whom played an important role in this book. Thank you!

Contents

What Others are Saying About Patti's First Book

"How to Ditch Your Allowance and Be Richer Than Your Parents"

Age is no barrier to wealth. "How to Ditch Your Allowance & Be Richer Than Your Parents: 9 Wealth Building Tools to make a Teen Rich" is a guide to being an entrepreneurial young man or woman who wants to plan wisely for the future. Explaining such concepts of wise money management, investing, and how to realize that not all debt is bad debt, "How to Ditch Your Allowance & Be Richer Than Your Parents" is an ideal guide for young adults.

Midwest Book Review

Patti Handy has written a winner! Purchasing this book for your teens is an investment in their future and a gift that will keep on giving.

As an author on rapid debt elimination myself, I often receive requests from parents asking if I have written anything for teens. Parents want to prevent their children from experiencing a debt-plagued life.

Since I have not done so, I highly recommend this book by Patti. I have read all the books on finances for teens and this one is the BEST!

Bruce Ammons
Author, The DEBTonator Course

An excellent book worth every penny and written in a conversational and easy-to-understand style. I learned as much as my daughter did! This is a MUST-READ for anyone who has every answered the question, "Can I have my allowance?"

Jane S.

Patti Handy may be a Cash Coach for Teens, however her advice is sound for all age groups. I ordered her book in hopes that it would help me educate my children in sound money management. The book came yesterday and I read it cover to cover last night. "How to Ditch Your Allowance.." is chalk full of sound advice. The wealth building tools and "advice from mom" went beyond my expectations and will most certainly help my children as then implement these tactics and techniques.

Thank you Patti for sharing your insights with us!

Ron D.

This type of information should be a required read in school! Money 101! Written in an easy to read, raw basics style, my kids had no problem absorbing it. It has sparked lively conversations about money and both my kids are now asking questions about careers, incomes and investing. I am thrilled to see they are pondering these topics when daydreaming (as opposed to video games and boys).

I highly, highly recommend it!

Eric L.

This is the kind of book I wish I had when I was a kid. The government should automatically hand this book to every teenager, and it should be mandatory reading material in junior high school and every few years thereafter. Frankly, anyone can benefit from this book, no matter what age. Patti's style is so friendly, and she demystifies what can be an overwhelming subject matter. This material should not be learned haphazardly as most of us tend to learn it. It is so much better to learn these fundamentals well before applying for a credit card or cashing a first paycheck. I certainly learned a thing or two ...or three! Patti has a knack for explaining financial concepts like stocks and bonds in such an accessible manner. Near the end of the book, Patti makes it clear that giving back is just as important and taking it in. People are often afraid of dealing with their finances, because no one ever teaches them what to do. This book empowers the reader. A great book at any age.

Robert Mansour, Esq.

I do not consider myself a "money" person and yet I found this book to be an informative, engaging read. The author introduces basic wealth building tools in a language that any teen or even pre-teen can understand. Her message is clear: achieving financial freedom is significantly more meaningful than image or accumulating material things (a lesson so many young people have yet to grasp). "This is not just about material wealth," she tells us, "but also about spiritual and emotional wealth." I will definitely share this book with my children, nieces and nephews.

Caradawn H.

I just finished reading this book and felt compelled to share my excitement for this fabulous book! As a loving parent of three kids, I have felt I failed miserably in teaching my kids to be fiscally responsible. Yet, I didn't know how to go about teaching them about financial health, until now! Patti Handy has written a book that is just what I needed to complete my parenting skills.

I found the book entertaining, educational and enlightening! Handy perfectly balances humor with her expertise to provide the reader with information in a manner that is not overwhelming. Her ability to share some much information in a clear concise manner is very effective. I certainly learned things as I read it (bull and bear markets, never knew the definition). The book is easily read by both my 17-year-old son, and 14-year-old daughter.

What I found the most impressive is the loving messages she extends to her son through the book, which also serve to anyone who reads the book. Because I live with an "attitude of gratitude", I am thrilled to read the passages that impart that philosophy to the reader.

The message that money is not just about the "toys" and the importance of "giving back" are vital to overall financial health and true inner happiness.

What a powerful tool you have provided us parents who are dedicated to helping our teens prosper.

I have tremendous respect and admiration for author Patti Handy!

Tami S.

I had the privilege of reading Patti Handy's book. As a CPA and a father, I think it should be required reading for every teenager. Patti's conversational style of presentation gives the feeling you have had a valuable talk with your favorite aunt. The fact that the information is presented is such a comfortable manner does not diminish at all from the valuable lessons to be learned. This book will help anyone be a much better manager of money. Those of my generation feel social security will most likely not be available when we need it; if today's generation heed Patti Handy's lessons, they won't care.

Peter M.

A Letter for the Parent ...

As of this writing, my son is 20. The teenage years have been interesting, to say the least. I totally get what you are experiencing. I am not out of the woods yet either.

One of my biggest personal struggles has been with communication, or lack thereof. I try, every single day, to have a conversation with my son. I ask questions and try to be a good listener. I ask about school, friends, work, etc. I also share my stories, as I want him to know I understand.

Some days he is more communicative than others are, but I will not ever stop asking questions.

I will share a little bit of my story with you. When my son was 18 months old, my husband asked for a divorce. To say I was blindsided and devastated would be an understatement. I was afraid, an emotional mess and completely stuck. My life was turned upside down in a matter of minutes.

The following weeks were a blur, as I struggled to pick up the pieces of my heart. As much as I wanted to stay in bed all day, I had a little guy who depended on me. He has been my greatest strength and my weakest link.

In the midst of this chaos, there was a sense of peace, knowing I could take care of myself financially. Not because I had a high paying job. I actually left my banking career to stay at home with my son. So, at the time, I was unemployed.

Here's the thing; I knew how to make, manage, save, invest and respect money. None of this came from my years in the banking world. This knowledge was a gift from my parents, as I was taught money smarts at a very young age.

So, why do I share this? I want this knowledge for your kids. We don't know what life will throw at them, but this life skill may help carry them through some difficult times.

Like you, there is nothing I will not do for my child. I want nothing more than to watch him become a happy, healthy, independent, compassionate and loving adult. He is well on his way, and I am incredibly proud and blessed.

Part of my responsibility in raising him is to make sure he is equipped with life skills to live a happy and joyful life. Most life skills are not taught in schools (a pet peeve... do not get me started), so it's up to me to teach them. Life skills such as how to treat people, kindness, serving, respect, work ethics, working smart and, of course, money smarts. (The list is much longer, as a parent, you know this.)

Money education isn't an option and it's up to us, as parents, to make sure our kids know how money works, the do's and do nots and why this is important. As I discuss, it's not about acquiring material items. It's about living a peaceful and generous life.

For many parents, having a conversation with their teens can be a challenge. I understand. Throw "money" into the equation, and the eyes begin to roll.

Maybe you have younger kids too. The tools in this book will help you start early, which is even better!

The great thing about this book is it can be used in two ways. You, as the parent, can read this book now and start the conversation with your kids. The information is plentiful and simple to understand.

The other way to use this book is to simply hand it to your teen. It is written for, and to the teen/twenty something in your life. The language is easy to understand, and hopefully a bit entertaining.

Better yet, give one copy to your child and keep a copy for yourself. Take notes, scribble in it and use as a resource for later. Encourage your child to do the same, in their book.

I know you, as a parent, want the same happy and joyful life for your kids. I hope this book will help you on that journey. Thank you for allowing me to be a part of your world. I invite you to sign up to my newsletter at www.teenscashcoach.com to stay in touch and read my blog.

Free Bonus!

Email Patti to receive the "action item" worksheets you find in this book!

A great way to complete them without writing in the book!

Patti@teenscashcoach.com

My gift to you!

A Letter for the Teen ...

Why you will want to read this book ...

Chances are you received this book from someone who cares deeply for you. It may be a parent, grandparent, aunt, uncle or maybe a teacher. Maybe I gave it to you.

I am going to guess this book was not on your top list of 'books I really want to read,' but I'm hoping when you are done you'll thank that wonderful person that gave it to you.

Why?

Because you'll learn some pretty cool money skills and habits that will help you experience a financially and emotionally peaceful life. Why is that important?

Well...

Are you tired of being frustrated with feeling broke? Stressed about not having money in the bank, or worse, not understanding money? I am here to help fix this.

None of what I share is difficult to understand and I don't plan on giving you a test on the material. For that reason, don't read it for any other reason than you want to learn. You want to fully embrace this beautiful gift called life.

So, let's talk about that.

What's your definition of a financially successful life? It is different for everyone and there really is not a right or wrong answer. It's personal.

For me, "financially successful" is a place where you don't stress about money. You're able to give freely to those in need and you're able support your family. You donate regularly; you pay your bills easily and save every single month. You can breathe…and sleep without worry. In addition, retirement does not scare you; it excites you.

It may be hard to think about retirement at your young age, but I'm here to tell you, it is never too early to think about it. And it sneaks up on you!

I want you to live comfortably. I'll bet the person who gave you this book wants the same for you, also.

Let's talk about another point…your WHY.

Why is money smarts and living financially free important to you? You have to tie it to an emotional reason. Your WHY shouldn't be a big house, a fancy car or expensive clothes.

Don't get me wrong, there's nothing wrong with wanting a nice home, car or clothes. But that can't be the main reason you want to be wealthy. There is a temporary satisfaction from a material item. It's a quick fix, but those "things" will not bring you a lifetime of happiness. There are countless millionaires who are miserable.

At this time in your life, depending upon your age, your goal may be to buy a car-any car! It may be to buy a new computer or to help pay for college. Something has to motivate you to stay on track. Start thinking about the long term too.

Maybe you have a passion for rescuing animals or working with kids. Maybe you do not know your WHY yet, and that is perfectly okay. I suggest you start thinking about it though. Have fun with the process-don't make it a chore.

In this book, I'm going to share tips and tools to help you create wealth. Not just financial wealth, but emotional wealth. We'll talk about personal development and the importance and power of your brain.

We will discuss how to use a credit card the right way, how to build your credit and why that is important. I will share some basic investment choices for you, some cool saving strategies and why you need to give your money away.

Yes, you read that right. You'll be learning great money smarts to help you create wealth, so you can share it with the world. That, my friend, is the key to happiness.

I'll also share some random "mom tips"- most of which have nothing to do about money, but everything to do about you.

I once heard someone say, "money and health...it's all you can think about if you do not have it." My thoughts exactly.

Now, let's get started so you can start living with abundance, peace and generosity!

1

Your Magnificence and Your Mindset

"Everything you want is on the other side of fear."

Jack Canfield

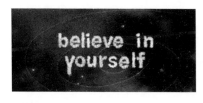 Let's get one thing perfectly clear here. You are magnificent. Every ounce of you, inside and out, is a work of art. You are brilliant.

There is no doubt you have talent, skill and a gift to share with the world. You may or may not see it, but it is there. Those who know you, see it. The question is, do you see it?

The only limitation you have is the limitation in your mind. Your amazing mind.

I do not care (well, I do, but I am trying to make a point here) where you are at in life. It does not matter where you live, how much money you have or don't have, where your parents live, or any other external factor.

I'm not talking about an academic brilliance either. There are tens of thousands of people in the world that did not do well in school, but went on to do amazing things in their life. Do you know the story behind Albert Einstein? Look it up. It will make you smile.

I love this quote from Henry Ford- **"Whether you think you can, or think you can't, you are correct."**

So, what do you think? Can you? Stand up right now and declare that YOU CAN!! Seriously, do it now.

Let's take this one step further...

With all your brilliance and talent, what do you want out of life? I'm not necessarily asking you what career path you want to take; I'm asking what you want out of life. Meaning, how do you want to make a difference in the world? What problem do you want to solve to help others? What type of lifestyle do you want to live? Where do you want to live? Do you have an idea what your purpose may be?

There's a quote I love from Mark Twain-**"The two most important days in your life are the day you are born and the day you find out why."** Go find out why.

It's okay if you don't have the answers to these questions right now, but start thinking about them. Have fun with the process and don't limit yourself.

Here are some suggestions to start thinking about this, including designing the life of your dreams. I highly suggest you write everything down and don't keep ideas and thoughts in your head. Writing thoughts down help you process and organize.

Think about the purpose of your life. This may seem heavy, and you may have no idea. Again, it's totally ok. Just start thinking about it.

What do you want in each area of your life?

- Financial
- Career
- Health - Physical and Mental
- Relationships
- Spiritual
- Contribution

Ask yourself "why are these important to me?"

What habits and beliefs/thoughts must you develop to achieve success in these areas of your life?

Keep a journal or notebook and write ideas down as they pop into your head. Start with the basic questions mentioned above and grow from there. Enjoy the process and don't place any limits on yourself.

Let's discuss your mind; the absolutely amazing mind and the power it holds.

Let me break this down: your mind has both a conscious and subconscious. Your conscious mind is the intellectual part that accepts or rejects ideas. It reasons and thinks. It says yes and no. Your conscious mind is your aware mind. You know exactly what you are doing.

Your subconscious mind cannot choose or reject a thought. It must accept any image and cannot differentiate between that which is real or imagined. The subconscious is truly amazing as it functions in every cell of your body. Your subconscious mind "tells" your heart to pump, your organs to function and self to breathe.

You may have heard about the natural laws of the universe. Once such law is "The Law of Perpetual Transmutation," which states, "The images you hold in your mind most often materialize as results in your life." You may have heard about the power of visualization—quieting your mind and seeing yourself doing or accomplishing something, feeling it with every emotion and playing it over and over in your mind. Many athletes use visualization techniques before competing in their sport.

Let me tie all this together.

So what does this conscious and subconscious mind stuff mean anyway? Here, in simple terms, is what happens: as a result of your thoughts and beliefs, you have certain feelings (emotions), which in turn move you to take certain actions, which then give you your results. So, if you do not like the results you see, whether it be money, career, relationship or health oriented, change your thoughts. Then take the proper action. (By the way, just thinking happy thoughts won't get the job done. You gotta put in the work).

Now, it's easier said than done to change our thoughts and beliefs. We have been programmed, and changing this requires some rewiring. That's where the subconscious comes in. There are countless books about the power of the mind, how it works, visualization techniques, the power of positive thinking, and the like.

My intention is not to give you the details of how the mind works in this book. I'll leave that to the experts. These people have spent decades studying the mind, how the conscious and subconscious work and have a far better understanding than I do. There is so much great material on the neuroscience of the brain that will blow you away! Go explore.

Here is what I want you to take away from this section. **Be mindful of your thoughts, for they will dictate the quality of your life.** I totally understand that we don't walk around every day, all day, in this happy go lucky state. That's unrealistic and just plain weird.

When you find yourself challenged or struggling with something, pay attention to what you're thinking. Really thinking. What's the belief system behind that thought? Do you believe in this belief or is this just ingrained in your mind since childhood? Did your parents respond this way too?

When it comes to money, here are some common limiting beliefs you may hear from others:

- Money is the root of all evil
- The rich get richer and the poor get poorer
- I am just not good with money
- My family has never been rich
- You have to work too hard to get wealthy
- You can be either rich or happy, not both
- It is selfish to want a lot of money

I suggest you ignore this negative noise. These beliefs are a reflection of others, their situations and their programmed belief.

I also believe that money makes you more of what you already are. If someone is greedy by nature, more money will make him or her greedier. On the other hand, if someone is generous by nature, money will make him or her more generous.

This mindfulness and awareness is the beginning of your shift. Be gentle with yourself, as a shift takes time. It will happen. Be patient.

One of the best ways that I have personally experienced staying positive is being *consciously grateful*. Make it a daily habit, either first thing in the morning or at bedtime, to take an inventory of all the wonderful things with which you are blessed.

Acknowledge everything and everyone, from your health, your family and friends, the love of your pet, the warmth and taste of hot cocoa, to the comfort of your pillow. Don't ever take any of it for granted and be eternally grateful.

Having this mindset, one of gratitude, will shift your focus to what is *right* in your world, rather than what is wrong. I call this a "gratitude adjustment."

Life will throw you curve balls that come in all forms. Whether it's health, financial, relationship, or career oriented, life will test you. Nobody said it was going to be easy. How you handle these challenges, by way of your perception and attitude will make a big difference in the quality of your life.

What I want for you is the mindset and understanding of how to help you through challenging times. Better yet, have this powerful and positive mindset all the time to maximize your experiences in life. I want you to embrace and enjoy life to the absolute fullest, no matter what is thrown your way.

You must stay positive, stay on course, step back for a moment, and look at the big picture. Don't let the outside world control you. That noise will distract and confuse you.

Affirmations are another way to stay on track with your mindset. By definition, an affirmation is "something declared to be true, a positive statement or judgment." In simple terms, an affirmation is a statement, spoken in present tense, which is both personal and positive. Here are a few examples:

"I am enjoying a beautiful life."

"I am doing what I love to do, while money flows to me."

"I am healthy and strong."

"My family and friends are enjoying abundance."

"I am making a difference in the world, doing what I love."

When you repeat these affirmations, close your eyes, visually see — and feel — what this looks like. Experience it as if it were happening this minute. Let your mind and body fully embrace this moment. Bring your emotions into this experience. This is where the subconscious rewiring takes place. You need to make this a daily habit for positive change to take place. Doing this every once in a while, won't cut it. Statistics show that repeating a behavior or thought for twenty-one days will create a new habit.

Nobody can take away your brilliance, talents, or skills. You should stay focused on your dreams and goals, regardless of the negativity that may surround you. This will not always be easy, but I know you can do it. Perseverance is key.

I know school and outside responsibilities can seem overwhelming at times. This mindset will help you through those times. Stay mindful: stay grateful.

Action Items

List three limiting beliefs that you presently have.

_____

_____

_____

Write out five positive affirmations that you will start to use daily.

_____

_____

_____

_____

_____

Take an inventory of where you are today about your money, relationships, career, spiritual place, health and contribution. List out where you are today in each of these areas. Then, write out where you want to be in 5 years, 10 years and 20 years from now, in these same areas. (You will probably need additional paper for this)

_____

_____

_____

_____

_____

_____

_____

_____

Describe in detail WHY this is important to you. What is your dream? Why is this important? Remember, your WHY cannot be attached to a material item.

_____
_____
_____
_____
_____
_____
_____
_____

List 3-5 people that you consider a positive role model or mentor/coach.

_____
_____
_____
_____
_____

Now, make a plan to reach out to them and share this information. Let them know you would love their help in your journey.

2

Will You Be Using Debit or Credit?

"It's failure that gives you the proper perspective on success."

Ellen DeGeneres

 Ahh, that little plastic card. What would life be like without it? I guess it depends on how you use it. This chapter will guide you on how to use credit wisely, explore the pros and cons of credit cards, and tell you how to stay out of hot water.

Let's start by explaining the difference between a credit card and a debit card. Both are plastic cards that look very similar and can be swiped to purchase something, but they are very different. Credit accounts typically cannot be opened until you are eighteen years old, but debit cards can be received earlier. Check with your bank or credit union for their minimum age requirements.

Debit cards

A debit card, which is also used as an ATM card, takes money out of your checking account much like writing a check does. Consider it immediate. The debit card is typically tied to your checking account, so any activity with your card affects your account balance immediately.

When you purchase something, and swipe your debit card, you must *always* write that purchase down just as if you wrote a check. You need to be certain to keep the running balance in your account, because if you overdraft (spend more than you have in the account), you will pay some ugly fees.

Some banks will not approve the transaction if you do not have enough money in the account, while I have seen some banks allow the transaction, but then slap you with an overdraft fee. Be sure to check with your bank as to their policy, but regardless, always know your present balance. Ask them to flag your account, so that any purchase made is denied, assuming you do not have the funds to cover the transaction. It's better to have the purchase denied, than pay an overdraft fee. You work way too hard to donate money to your bank in fees. There are many great apps that help you keep track of your expenditures, so there are no excuses.

When you need to take cash out of your account, you would use that debit card at the ATM (automated teller machine). Again, make sure you make note of your cash withdrawal on whatever system you use for tracking. Maybe it is an old-fashioned check register!

I have heard some people say, "Why was I able to make that purchase if I didn't have the money in my account? Why would the bank let that purchase go through?" First, it is your responsibility to manage your money, not the bank. Second, the bank profits from the fees they charge you. Track, track, track your spending!

On to the credit cards

When you use a credit card, think, "borrow." If you use a credit card to purchase something and do not pay off the balance in full when your bill arrives, think "bad debt." There, I am done.

Before I go into details and examples, understand this bottom line: credit cards, if used incorrectly, will wreak havoc on your life. Getting out from under credit card debt is very difficult and extremely stressful. Once the snowball starts, it can be quite the challenge to demolish. It can take years and years to pay off credit, which means the $75 pair of jeans or $350 cell phone can cost you far more than the original purchase price.

When you purchase something using a credit card, the charge is not deducted from your checking account like a debit card. With a credit card, your purchases are accumulated, and then you will receive a monthly bill. When that monthly bill lands in your lap, hopefully you are not surprised with "wow, things sure do add up."

My guess is those words will come out of your mouth on a few occasions. I know they have for me. They do for everybody, so don't beat yourself up for it. The important thing is what you do next.

If you pay the bill in full, and on time, you generally will not be charged any interest. There should not be any finance charges and if you pay on time, there will not be any late fees. You have been able to "borrow" money without any charges for a short period of time for free.

Be careful here though and watch the due date. The billing cycle will vary from card to card, which means if you have more than one credit card, they will typically be due on different days.

When you receive your bill in the mail, you will be given the option to make a minimum payment. Taking this option is a huge mistake. *Do not pay just the minimum payment.* If you do not pay the bill in full, you will incur interest or finance charges, and, if the bill is paid late, some late fees.

If you go over your limit on the card, you will get slapped with an additional fee, too. Yikes. To add salt to the wound, if you go over your limit, many banks may raise the interest rate on your card and you will not be able to lower it again. Talk about a costly mistake! As you fall behind in payments, your credit scores will be hurt in the process, too. The chapter on credit scores will go into this subject in depth.

I will share some startling numbers with you in a moment—the true cost of an item if put on credit cards and not paid in full.

The good part …

Having said all that, credit card usage, if done correctly, will help you build a credit history, will help increase your credit scores, and is quite convenient. There are many pros to having credit cards.

If you are in a pinch or in an emergency situation, a credit card can be a lifesaver. (I am not talking about *needing* those new shoes here.) If you need your car towed, run out of gas, have a medical emergency, or any other type of unexpected surprise expense, a credit card is a godsend.

Credit cards are also easier to use when you travel, eliminating the need to carry cash. If cash is stolen, you are done. If your card is stolen, you can get a replacement quickly and not be on the hook for charges that are not yours. Just be sure to call the credit card company immediately.

Here is another cool fact about using credit …many credit cards offer cash back, points for traveling or other types of great rewards! I know people who have traveled extensively using points for plane flights and hotel, which means it does not cost them hard-earned cash to see the world!

When you use your credit card, you earn points on purchases, which accumulate over time. These points can mean cash towards future purchases or credit towards hotels, flight costs and more.

Shop online for which offers interest you the most. Please watch interest rates and terms of this service. Read the fine print and make sure you understand what you are getting into.

Be careful not to overextend, just to earn points. Follow the same rules of using credit wisely!

Some tips to keep in mind …

There are some smart ways to use cards and some things to look out for. These tips will guide you along the way.

When you get your first credit card, I recommend a low credit limit, such as $300. This means that you are not able to spend more than $300 on your card before paying some of it down. It acts like a ceiling for you. This way you can learn to manage buying and paying, without the risk of getting too deep. As you become more comfortable with using the card, you can request a higher credit limit. Take this responsibility seriously, as mistakes or misuse can affect your credit history for years. As I have mentioned, your credit history can save you (good credit scores) or cost you dearly (poor credit scores) over time.

When you are ready for your first card, try to get a VISA, MasterCard, or Discover. The credit bureaus look more favorably on these. I prefer this type of card over department stores, as department stores typically have higher interest rates and you may tend to have more impulse purchases at department stores, knowing you have that credit card. You can use the VISA/MasterCard anywhere, including department stores. Sometimes, starting out, it may be hard to get a bank card (VISA/MasterCard), so I would suggest you get a gas card. You need to put gas in your car anyway, so use this card and pay in full, to establish some credit history.

Find a bank that does not charge an annual fee. Some banks will charge you an annual fee and some will not. If your bank charges you one, tell them you will not open a card unless they waive that fee, forever. There are plenty of places you can go and get that fee waived. Everything is negotiable.

Protect yourself by taking a few precautions when using your debit or credit cards. You will be asked to choose a PIN number on your debit card. PIN stands for Personal Identification Number. Be sure to memorize it and do not share with anyone. Pick a number that would be hard to guess, not your birthday or year of birth. Even your phone number or address should be avoided. Do not write this number down and leave in your wallet or in a location that is easily accessible. This PIN number will be asked of you (you will enter on a keypad, never give this to an employee) when you withdraw cash from an ATM or make a payment with your debit card.

Make sure to review the charge amount when you are making the purchase on your credit card and keep your receipts. You will want to cross check the receipts against the credit card bill to be sure there were not any mistakes. Everyone makes mistakes, so be sure to take the time to check your statements completely. You may even find a charge the bank charged you that should not be there. If this happens, call the bank and get that charge reversed from (taken off) your bill.

When shopping for a credit card, be aware of the details: specifically, whether the interest rate is variable or fixed, what the interest rate is, and if they are teasing you with an introductory rate. Obviously, the lower the interest rate, the better. A fair interest rate is between 5% and 11% but can go much higher; anything higher should be avoided. Keep in mind the interest rate only comes into play if you do not pay your credit card in full. If you pay in full every month, the interest rate is not important. You should still strive for the lowest rate in case you have to carry a balance for a short time. As with everything, this rate is negotiable. If the credit card company starts to move this rate up on you, get on the phone with them and tell them you will take your business elsewhere unless they work with you. There are some student credit cards available, with nice benefits and services, so be sure to take the time to do your homework. Always review your statement for interest rate changes.

If your bank offers you a credit card with an *introductory rate*, run, do not walk. This means they will play nice for one year or so, and then make you want to cry. The best-case scenario is the lowest *fixed rate* you can find. Avoid variable interest rate cards as well. Make sure to read the fine print so you know what you are getting yourself into. Here again, doing your homework will save you lots of money over time.

What does it really cost you?

As I have mentioned, if you do not pay your credit card off in full every month, you will incur an interest expense, and, if late, a late fee. For this example, let's just look at the interest expenses.

Let's say you decide you must have the latest cell phone. You did not want to wait until you had the cash in hand. Let's say that cell phone was $500, and you decided to charge the amount. I will give you a couple different scenarios of what that cell phone costs you and how long it would take you to pay it off, assuming you only paid the minimum amount.

Credit card balance	Interest rate	Minimum	Interest cost	Months to pay off
$500	20%	$25	$113	25

In this example, you would have paid $613 for that cell phone, not $500, and it would have taken you over two years to pay it off. My guess is by that time, a newer phone would have become available. Keep in mind; this does not take into consideration any late fees that may have been incurred as well.

Let's look at a few more examples:

Credit card balance	Interest rate	Minimum	Interest cost	Months to pay off
$1,000	18%	$50	$198	24
$2,000	18%	$100	$396	24
$2,000	20%	$50	$1,323	67

Did you catch that last one? It would take you almost 5½ years to pay this off and cost you an additional $1,323 by paying the minimum only payment. Talk about crazy!

The minimum payment is typically calculated at 5% of outstanding balance (as of this writing), but can differ. The above scenarios are for instructional purposes only.

Here is something very important I want you to remember. You do not necessarily need to go out and buy one large ticket item to bring your credit card debt up. Items add up quickly. One dinner out, one new pair of shoes, a must have pair of jeans, then some coffee stops with friends, a few movies out, some music downloads—you get the picture. A few dollars here and there add up to a boatload of moolah.

If you carry that balance to the next month, then make a few more purchases, suddenly it is very hard to catch up. This is how people get into serious trouble. Once that cycle begins, getting out from underneath that credit card debt is very difficult.

Ask yourself if the item is a *need* or a *want*. Depending upon the item, is it coming out of play money or short-term savings? Are your savings goals being met? Again, it is about being mindful.

Do not get me wrong here; I do not want to take the wind out of your sails. Making wise decisions when you are looking to purchase something can save you potentially thousands of dollars over time.

I want to take this one step further and show you some bigger credit card balances. Let us look at a few examples that will scare you enough to make the right choice.

Credit card balance	Interest rate	Minimum	Interest cost	Months to pay off
$5,000	18%	$100	$4,311	94

On this one, the interest alone costs you almost as much as the debt itself and will take you nearly eight years to pay off. Note: *your required minimum payment would probably be higher, but I wanted to illustrate how interest charges accumulate.*

Credit card balance	Interest rate	Minimum	Interest cost	Months to pay off
$5,000	18%	$500	$458	11

This shows how a higher monthly payment will reduce your interest expense and time to pay off. If you cannot pay in full, make the most payment, you possibly can to reduce interest.

There are some great calculators online that will allow you to put in different scenarios. Just search, "payment calculators" and you will find many options. The same goes for phone apps.

Please, please, please, only use credit when you know you have the cash to pay it off in full, unless it is an emergency. Think hard before you put anything on credit and do not let yourself fall into this money trap.

Action Items

Describe how a debit card is different from a credit card.

_____

_____

_____

_____

_____

When you use a debit card, when is the money withdrawn from your account?

_____

_____

_____

_____

_____

What does ATM stand for?

_____

What does PIN stand for? When would you use this?

_____

_____

What are some of the don'ts when using a debit card?

_____
_____
_____
_____
_____
_____

What are some of the don'ts when using a debit card?

_____
_____
_____
_____
_____
_____
_____
_____

List some of the ways that credit cards are used incorrectly

_____
_____
_____
_____
_____

What is the most important thing to do when using a credit card?

_____

_____

_____

Is it preferable to pay the minimum on a credit card bill?
Why or why not?

_____

_____

_____

_____

_____

_____

List three pros of credit cards:

_____

_____

_____

List two cons of credit cards

_____

_____

Describe what happens if you pay only the minimum on
your credit card bill

_____

_____

_____

What are three important lessons to remember when using credit cards?

_____

_____

_____

If you already have a credit card, what is the interest rate you are paying?

_____

3

Know Credit or No Credit

"I have not failed. I've just found 10,000 ways that do not work."

Thomas Edison

 In my book, *How to Ditch Your Allowance and be Richer Than Your Parents*, I covered this topic at great length. This topic is so important, I decided to include it in this book, with very few changes. Please make sure you understand your credit and take managing it very seriously. You may not necessarily appreciate this now, but I guarantee you, you will in the very near future.

Your credit score, also called a FICO score, is, in simple terms, very similar to your grades in school. *FICO is a credit score developed by Fair Isaac Corp, a company that specializes in*

what's known as "predictive analytics," which means they take information and analyze it to predict what's likely to happen.[1]

You are *graded* based on your performance and abilities. In this case, your performance is related to your ability to manage credit. Credit can come in the form of a credit card, a car loan, a mortgage, or a personal loan.

In my line of work as a Mortgage Advisor, I see credit reports every day. I also see the difference in interest rates that I can offer a client who has a score of 712 versus someone who has a score of 740.

Such a small difference, you may say, but what is shocking is the difference of total interest one will pay over time, given the two FICO scores. Needless to say, stay on top of your credit or it will cost you dearly.

Credit scores range from 300–850. So, what's a good score? Well, it depends on whom you ask. Most would agree that an excellent score is 740 or above. Consider this an A in school. Anything below 620 is considered poor, or risky. A score of 700–740 is generally considered good, while 680–700 is fair.

If I were the teacher, I would give the following grades:

A   740+
B   700–740
C   680–700

---

[1] https://www.credit.com/

D   620–680
F   620 or below

When you get your own credit card, it is your sole responsibility to pay that bill on time and preferably pay it in full, every single month. (If you know you cannot pay the bill in full, you should not make that purchase. A few exceptions are allowed, such as an emergency- I made this crystal clear earlier.) Making those payments on time, and in full, is like turning in A work at school.

Who gives these scores to you anyway?

The most widely used credit scores are FICO scores, which were created by Fair Isaac Corporation. Lenders buy the scores from three major credit-reporting agencies. The three major credit-reporting agencies in the U.S. are, Experian, Equifax, and TransUnion.

These agencies maintain your credit records and other information about you. The records are called your credit report, and this report is what lenders look at before they decide to give you credit. Your credit score will also determine the interest rate and other terms of your loan. Bad credit equals bad interest rate; good credit equals good interest rate. You will save big money over time if you have a lower interest rate. This is why you must keep your credit scores high and take responsibility when using credit. Again, it will cost you dearly if you do not.

What you can expect to find on your credit report...

Just as a report card will give you more than just your grades, your credit report gives more than just your credit score. There are all types of information about you on your report.

Here are the main sections:

- ID section
- Credit history section
- Collection accounts section
- Public records
- Additional information
- Inquiry section

ID section

In this section, you will find simple, basic information. Your name, address, social security number, date of birth and spouse's name (if applicable).

Credit history section

This section is the meat and potatoes of your report. It lists all your open and paid credit accounts. This section will give details such as company name, account number, whose account it is (if had joint or cosigner), date the credit was opened, the history on months reported, last activity information, terms, outstanding balance, high credit, past due and status. It will also list any late payment information.

Collection accounts section

This section is where you will find any accounts that went to collection. It is a good idea to keep your eyes on this section, as there might be something here that is not yours. Errors on credit reporting do occur, so keep tabs.

Public records

Here you will find a listing of public record items that are either, local, state or federal court related. A few examples include bankruptcy, tax liens, judgments, or collection accounts.

Additional information

This section discloses past addresses and previous employers.

Inquiry section

If any business has pulled your credit in the past twenty-four months, their name will appear here. Too many inquiries can harm your credit score, so do not give your authorization to pull credit unless it is absolutely necessary.

What factors go into your score?

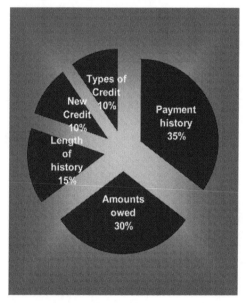

Let's break this down, while keeping it simple. I will give you the basic, important information you need to know. Credit scoring is complicated and the calculations remain a mystery.

Payment history accounts for 35% of your credit score. This tells us whether you have made your payments on time. As you can see, this weighs heavy on the score, as it accounts for 35%. Lenders want to know how responsible you are with managing money and your payments. Making one late payment is not an automatic score killer, but it will drop your score, so it's important to keep your bills organized and make sure nothing is overlooked. These payments can be on credit cards, car loans, any finance company or mortgage loans. I suggest you keep all your bills in one location and pay them twice per month, usually the first and fifteenth of the month. Watch the credit card due dates, as they will differ from card to card. If you wish, call the credit card companies and try to schedule the billing dates to be the same.

Amounts owed accounts for 30% of your credit score. Simply put, this looks at what you owe on credit as a percentage of the total credit available to you. To keep your scores up, maintain that percentage below 35%. For example, let us say you have a credit card with available credit of $1,000. If you use that card and your balance goes above approximately $350, your scores will be affected. In this example, keep the balance below $350. The credit bureaus do not like to see you "maxed out," as it implies you may not make your payment on time, if at all. Given this information, you may be tempted to run out and get a bunch of credit cards so you have a lot of *available* credit, but be careful. Too many cards can lower your score, as it increases risk. What is the magic number of cards? It depends. Start out with one or two major credit cards (AMEX, VISA, Discover or MasterCard). You can add a gas card or one department store card, but do not add more than one or two. Having three to five credit lines is enough, especially as a young adult. If you have a car loan, that would count as a credit line as well. More is not necessarily better with credit cards.

Length of credit history accounts for 15% of your credit score. The longer you have a credit history the better. This is why you do not want to close older credit cards, even if you do not use them. Cut them up and stop using them, just do not close the account. On the flip side, do not fret if you are new to credit and do not have much of a history. You can have good scores without history if the rest of your credit report looks good.

New credit accounts for 10% of your credit score. Too much of a good thing is a bad thing. You shouldn't go out and open a bunch of new accounts at once. It signals that you may be overextending yourself, or worse, are already in trouble. Also, newer accounts will lower your average account age, which will have a large impact if you do not have other credit information. This ties in with the previous section on length of credit history.

Types of credit accounts for 10% of your credit score. Simply stated, mix it up. Your score will improve if you have a healthy mix of credit. For example: credit cards, school loans, installment loans (car payment), and mortgage loans. Remember, more is not necessarily better.

So, why the big deal?

As I mentioned early on, the credit score calculations are complicated and much goes into them. I have discussed the primary, most important aspects of your score. Why are they so important? What is the best way to get good scores?

For starters, many people, not just lenders or car financing companies, look at your credit scores.

Some employers will look at your credit scores to determine how responsible you are. Doesn't it make sense that if you are responsible with managing your money, you would be responsible as an employee? I think it makes total sense.

Some insurance companies will also look at scores to determine pricing on your policies. Talk about a costly mistake if you let your scores drop. If you decide to rent an apartment or home before buying, landlords will pull credit to determine if they want to rent to you, or not. It can be a risky proposition for them if your scores are poor. On the flip side, if you have excellent scores and are competing with another person for that rental, you may win.

When it comes time to buy your first car, finance a big purchase, or buy your first home, your credit score will dictate the interest rate you pay. It will cost you dearly if you have poor credit. In some cases, you will not be able to get credit at all if the scores are too low. I cannot stress enough how important it is to be on your game with your credit.

As a note, I do not suggest you finance big purchases. When it comes time to buy furniture, a laptop, or similar big-ticket items, pay cash. If you cannot pay cash, wait until you can. Feel free to put it on a credit card only if you know you will pay it off in full when the bill arrives.

Tip: If you have an issue getting your first credit card, you have a few options. One is a "prepaid credit card." With this, you prepay the bank for the credit limit on your card. You will pay the bank, say $300, for a $300 prepaid card. I know, you are thinking, "if I have the cash, I'll just pay cash," but this allows you to build credit.

Your second option is become an "authorized user" on another person's card, probably your parents. The upside? You benefit from their credit history and have a credit card. The downside? If you mess up, your credit AND your parent's credit suffer. Take this privilege, and responsibility, very seriously.

How to get a copy of your credit report

As of this writing, you are allowed to pull your own credit report once per year for free. If you pull it yourself, it will not count as an inquiry on your report, which is preferable. Go to www.annualcreditreport.com for the free report. If you want your scores, you will have to pay a nominal fee. You can also order your credit report directly from the credit reporting agencies. Here is their contact info:

Equifax: www.equifax.com   800-685-1111

Experian: www.experian.com   888-397-3742

TransUnion: www.transunion.com   800-888-4213

If you ever find an error on your report, you would need to contact the above agencies to dispute. If you report an error to the agency, they must investigate and respond to you within thirty days.

How to get credit scores up and keep them up

Here are a few suggestions for getting those scores up:

- Keep balances low on credit cards and other revolving credit. (Remember the amount owed I mentioned?)

- Do not close those cards that you do not use, especially if they are older cards. Cut them up and stop using them, just leave them open.

- Do not open a bunch of new credit cards that you do not need just to increase available credit. That could backfire on you.

- Pay your bills on time, pay your bills on time, and always remember to *pay your bills on time*. I realize that was annoying, but I want that stuck in your brain.

- When it's time to buy your car or home, shop for the loan within a short period of time, preferably two to three weeks. Each inquiry will not be considered a single inquiry this way.

- When the nice person at the department store offers you 10% off your purchase if you open a credit card, smile and say, "No, thank you."

Unless you need the credit, do not open just to open.

- Using credit cards to pay for gas or food, knowing you will pay that off in full, will help raise your score. Showing that you can *use and pay* on a regular, consistent basis will exhibit responsible behavior.

- Never go over your credit limit. The credit card companies will allow you to do that sometimes, but your scores will drop, as you will be maxed out.

- If any of this is confusing and overwhelming, don't fret. You're not alone. Just make sure you educate yourself before making any decisions and don't be pressured into anything.

- If all else fails, call someone experienced whom you trust.

I realize this was a lot of information to take in one sitting. Use this as a reference and reread it as necessary. Getting on top of your credit and staying on top of it will benefit you more than you realize. You truly will not appreciate this until you have experienced life a little.

Action Items

When you get a credit card, why is it a good idea to start with a low limit?

_____

_____

_____

_____

_____

Why or why not is it a good idea to apply for those clothing store credit cards when they offer you 10% discount when you open a new account?

_____

_____

_____

_____

_____

What type of credit card is best to start out with?

_____

_____

_____

_____

_____

What is a fixed rate and what is an introductory rate? Which is better and why?

_____

_____

_____

_____

_____

How many credit cards/credit lines are best?

_____

_____

_____

_____

_____

What is the best way to build a good credit history?

_____

_____

_____

_____

_____

_____

_____

_____

_____

_____

Name the three credit bureaus

_____

_____

_____

Why is a good credit score important? Who looks at your credit?

_____

_____

_____

_____

_____

4

Mom's Mini Life Lessons

"Success is not final, failure is not fatal:
it is the courage to continue that counts."
Winston Churchill

 This chapter may seem completely random, because it is. These are important for life balance and I have a desire to share them, so please indulge me.

As a mom of a 20 year old myself, I've had many years of practice being a parent. And I'm still learning how to parent. I make mistakes all the time, but I try hard to learn from them. Sometimes I make the same mistake more than once, which really hurts. For both of us.

As in life, I get knocked down, but I always get up. You will experience the same, I am sure.

Here are a few tidbits that I have shared with my son over the years, which I thought you might enjoy. They do not have much to do about financial wealth, but more of emotional wealth.

I'm a sponge when it comes to personal development subjects. I believe if I'm not moving forward, I'm moving backward. So, I read, listen to experts and just try to become a better person by understanding human nature. It's also something I love as a Life Coach.

Of course, I get excited about what I learn and want to share it with my son. "If I knew this stuff growing up, it would have been great!" I think to myself. I have to share this!

In my excitement or passion, I sometimes find myself 'fire hosing' him.

I hope the sprinkles of what I share impact him, and you, in the long term.

Make it a point every day to show kindness to someone. Everybody has a story and everybody is struggling with something in his or her lives. Always be compassionate and understanding of this and never judge others.

This is one of my mini life lessons. The cool thing is I see him doing this. Every time we pass a homeless person, he wants to buy them food. He loves babies and kids and treats them so sweetly. I love it.

Here is one I used when he was entering high school. I knew these times might be challenging, as he navigates peer pressure, girls (possible rejection) and just figuring himself out.

I can't protect you from all the hurts or pains you will go through, but I promise you that I will always be here for you. As painful as life lessons are, they will make you a better person.

You can't control what people say to you or how they treat you, but you can control your reaction to it. Don't give anyone your power by letting them make you feel a certain way. Be proactive, not reactive.

Remember this important question: since when did someone else's opinion about you become more important than your opinion of yourself? You realize their opinion is a reflection of "their issues." Whatever struggles, challenges or issues they have within themselves, they will reflect onto others. Remember this too, when you may judge others. What is going on within you? Self-reflection is important, even if it hurts.

No matter how bad things may seem at times, remember it is only temporary. You won't feel this way forever.

When my son started to drive, I was freaked out. I still remember the first time he pulled away from the house, on his own. It took everything in my power not to completely lose it. I had to trust, let go and let him hit the road on his own.

I remember telling him this during this time…

Don't ever drive when you're angry. You will drive fast and reckless and get in an accident. Don't give anyone that power over you, no matter how angry or heartbroken you may feel. Take time to cool off and gather your thoughts before getting behind the wheel.

We had the conversations about texting and driving, drinking and driving and general "do not let your friends distract you while you're driving" as well. Please take this seriously and do not text and drive, drink and drive or drive distracted. Your life, and others, are at stake.

Even now, years later, I still worry when he is on the road. It's crazy out there and it's not just about his driving, it's about all the other boneheads on the road. I have always told him, "It's about being a defensive driver that will keep you from getting in an accident."

I'm sure your parents say the same thing to you. They are right - listen to them.

Always take responsibility for your actions or behavior. Meaning, when you do something and it doesn't work, take responsibility and make the necessary changes. Don't blame or waste your time trying to find fault in others. If you've done something, anything, in life that was a mistake, acknowledge it and then change it. Own it, then make it right. This can be applied to both your personal life and professional life. (Your future spouse will appreciate me for that recommendation.)

Be aware of your imperfections. Everyone on this planet has strengths and weaknesses. Nobody is a saint, nobody is perfect. Do not expect that of yourself. Accept and embrace your strengths and weaknesses and be confident in your ability to solve whatever problems that may occur. I have total confidence in you.

Remember to dream. Dream big. Let your imagination soar and think about what it is you want to do with your life. What type of profession would make you incredibly happy, while serving the world? Set some goals for yourself, incorporating your dreams. Make sure and write those goals down on paper.

Stay organized. Keep papers, receipts, contracts, and legal documents in a central location or file. Know where everything is at all times. Staying organized will keep the chaos at bay and keep you in control. Knowing you have a handle on paperwork will bring you a sense of peace with your personal and business matters. Keeping your bills in one location will minimize the chance of missing a payment, too. Getting in this habit at a young age will prove especially helpful as you get older. I realize this one was especially random, but it is important!

Thanks again for indulging me in this completely, out of the blue, chapter. My hope is that you were able to take a nugget or two from this.

I will end with one of my favorites…**Do not judge your insides by somebody else's outside!**

Action Items

Which one of these random 'mom' suggestions resonated with you? Why?

_____

_____

_____

_____

How do you handle life situations that knock you down?

_____

_____

_____

_____

_____

Are you happy with the way you handle those life situations you mentioned above? If not, how could you improve?

_____

_____

_____

_____

_____

_____

_____

_____

_____

How is your communication with your parent(s)? How can it improve?

_____

_____

_____

_____

_____

_____

_____

_____

_____

_____

_____

_____

_____

5

Say Yes to the Stress

"The only real mistake is the one from which we learn nothing."

Henry Ford

Stress sucks.

Or does it?

You are dealing with school, friends, maybe work and just juggling life. There are lots of tests, both in school and in everyday life. I get it.

According to Tess Cox, an Executive Coach and Consultant, stress is not all bad. In fact, "a healthy stress can help motivate us to make decisions, move forward and think more clearly." Whereas an unhealthy stress can cause anxiety, fear and anger, just to name a few familiar emotions.

When I feel the most stressed out, it usually comes back to me feeling out of control in some aspect of my life. My stress may have something to do with a current situation, but more times than not, it's future based.

When you are feeling stressed, Tess shares a few strategies that can help.

Start out by asking yourself, "is this stress good or negative?" Identify the stressors, specifically. Make a list of what is causing/creating the stress. I highly suggest writing it down on paper, not just verbally making the list. Something happens when you start writing.

- Are you worried about a test coming up in school?
- Are you feeling peer pressure to do something you know is wrong? (talk to parents!!)
- Are there issues with friends that are bothering you?
- Are there issues with your boyfriend/girlfriend?
- Trying to decide on a career choice?

Once the list is complete, review each item and ask "what can be done *today* to work through this?" Stay present. What choices can you make today to help tomorrow?

If the issue is homework related, breakdown what needs to be done, and by when. Learn to prioritize your obligations, much like life. Time management is crucial in life, both for kids and adults. This invaluable tool will help you throughout life, at any age. Trust me.

If you get caught up in the 'what-if's' of life, it can oftentimes paralyze you. We are living in the future and that can be exhausting. (Take it from me, I am pretty good at the 'what-if's', but I'm getting better).

One of the items Tess mentioned in our conversation that resonated with me was this: "we lead our emotions; emotions do not lead us." We are still in charge, even with emotions. When you are feeling stressed, with emotions running high, try to see this. It's very empowering!

Ask, "What's not working here?" Go deeper with each response. Then create a plan (again, I say written) to work through your specific challenges.

Have a conversation with your parents or a trusted adult. Talking things out always helps. Plus, they have experienced what you are experiencing. Remember, they were young once and went through these same stresses.

As you go deeper with questions, you will begin to discover you have the power to change your circumstances. This is where the shift begins and the magic starts to happen. Once you realize you have influence over your paradigm and actions, you begin to feel empowered. You feel back in control of the situation.

You must uncover what is causing the stress, and make sure there is not a deeper issue, such as bullying, substance abuse, peer pressure, deep anxiety or any other issue. Get help from a licensed therapist, reach out to family and friends and keep the communication open.

One of the most common stressors for teens is managing school and its demands. Time management is crucial, yet most teens struggle with this.

I suggest you do homework for 90 minutes, and then break for 30 minutes. After 90 minutes, your ability to absorb information starts to decrease, so take a break. Take a walk, listen to music or do whatever helps you relax.

I remember doing a version of this when my son was younger. I would have him work for 45 minutes, then break for 10. Little chunks of time helped him focus better.

Here are some additional tips that may help you deal with stress. All of these can be done in just a few minutes.

- **Take a snooze**. I love my power naps, when I can fit them in. I always feel refreshed and re-energized. Find a dark room and set your alarm for 15-30 minutes max. If you sleep too much longer than that, you may wake up feeling worse and it may affect your ability to fall asleep that night. Generally speaking, the best time to nap is between 1-3 p.m.

- **Exercise!** Find something you love to do, which will increase the odds of you sticking with it. Get the heart rate up and try to exercise a little every day. Even a 15-minute walk is beneficial. I suggest walking, running, weight training, martial arts, yoga, tennis or whatever you enjoy.

- **Just Breathe**. Sit comfortably, close your eyes and breathe from your belly. Put one hand on the lower abdomen and make sure you feel the belly rise and fall. Do not breathe from the chest. Take a few deep breaths and then slow the breathing down. Only a few minutes of this can help quiet the mind and reduce stress.

- **Visualizations**. This can sometimes be challenging, especially with our busy minds, but if you include all of your senses, it becomes easier. Visualizing will help our mind calm down and helps turn off our body's stress response. As I mentioned, use all senses. My happy place is the beach, so I visualize sitting on a comfy beach chair, looking out to the beautiful ocean. I feel my toes in the sand, I feel the wind blow across my hair and skin, I smell the salty ocean air, I hear the waves crashing to shore and I see the blue water with white caps. The more details the better. Define your happy place and, in detail, go there virtually.

- **Listen to music**. My son loves music that makes me crazy, but if it works for him, power to him. Whether it's rock and roll, pop, or simply the sound of nature, listening to music can help with stress. Have some good headphones so you do not make your family nutty. If you play a musical instrument, go play!

- **Organize, organize, and organize**. Personally, I love this one. Clutter makes me crazy and it's a fact that clutter causes stress and reduces productivity. That's not just me saying it, it is a proven fact! Clean up your room, clear off your desk and file papers away. Chaos creates chaos.

- **Eat healthy**. We all know we feel better when we eat right, so why do we eat junk food? Sugars and fats are especially evil. I have a sweet tooth, always have and probably always will. I can feel the difference when I have had too much sugar- it's not pretty. Do your best to stay away from fast food- most of it is full of fat and chemicals that do not serve your body well.

- **Progressive Muscle Relaxation**. This is simply 'tensing and relaxing' your muscles. I like to start with my head and work my way down to my toes. I tighten my skull (the best I can anyways, without making a scary face), then move down to my shoulders, arms, chest, stomach, etc. Tense and release each muscle and watch your body become calm and relaxed.

- **Positive thinking and self-talk**. Habit is key here. We must make it a habit to be kind to ourselves, with positive self-talk. If you are in the habit of being optimistic, whether it is about life's issues or any other challenges, you will be healthier, happier and most likely get better grades. Put post-it notes in your room or bathroom mirror with positive affirmations, which you can read every day.

The above suggestions are for those more common stress issues. If you struggle with deeper issues, such as depression or anxiety, please seek the help of a licensed therapist and talk to your parents.

The reality is we will always experience stress in our lives. There really is no way to escape it, regardless of how old you are, how rich you are or how successful you are. The trick is to learn how to reduce stress and cope with it.

At some points in our life, stress will be low, while other times, the fire will be burning high. Know that these high stress level times are temporary and how you address them will make a big difference in how you feel. Self-care is crucial as you face your issues head on.

Please avoid the temptation of turning to drinking, smoking, vaping or drugs. They may give you a temporary relief, but long term; you will be dealing with a far greater stress. Not only will these habits harm your body, they will in turn create health issues, which is the greatest stress of all.

We become our greatest when put to the test. We become stronger, wiser, kinder and more resilient as we work through our challenges. Think of a muscle that grows bigger and bigger-it happens by first being broken down and exhausted to complete fatigue, right? The same goes for the challenges you face in life. After you have worked that muscle to fatigue, what you feed your body afterwards will help that muscle grow bigger, or weaker. Feed your body well, both physically and emotionally.

You will face times when you may want to give up. You may think you can't do something or you are just plain exhausted. Don't give up. Don't ever give up. You are not alone in this experience. Everyone, and I mean everyone, has been here at some point in life.

Talk to family, friends, mentors or any trusted person in your life. You will get through these challenging times. I did, and so can you.

"Don't be afraid of pressure. Remember, pressure is what turns a piece of coal into a diamond." – Anonymous

Action Items

What are some of the major stressors in your life today?

_____

_____

_____

_____

_____

Given the stressors you mentioned above, do you consider them good or bad stressors?

_____

_____

_____

_____

_____

_____

What can be done today to work through this stress?

_____

_____

_____

_____

_____

Have a conversation with your parent(s) regarding the stress you are experiencing and write down your feelings and thoughts. Did this conversation help?

_____
_____
_____

What are some of your favorite ways to reduce stress? What activities helps you relax?

_____
_____
_____
_____
_____

6

Got Entrepreneurship?

"Every adversity, every failure, every heartache carries
with it the seed of an equal or greater benefit."
Napoleon Hill

This is one of my favorite topics to write and speak about. Why?

Because it empowers everyone to use their gifts, skills and talents to create an income and serve the world.

Win, Win!

If you're not quite old enough to have a job, or if you're having a hard time finding a job, this chapter will be especially helpful for you. I love the idea of sparking an entrepreneurial spirit in everyone, as the sky is the limit.

Don't get me wrong here; I am a HUGE advocate of college. In fact, you need a solid foundation that can be found in college to be successful as an entrepreneur. In fact, some universities offer a degree in Entrepreneurship! I love this.

Although being an entrepreneur is technically 'working for yourself,' this could not be farther from the truth. Yes, you are your own boss, you can make your own hours and there is no cap to your income.

Keep in mind, your clients/customers are your 'boss', you have to work many hours, especially at the beginning to build your business to be successful, and if you don't work, you don't get paid. This is not meant to freak you out or discourage you; I just want you to understand the reality of the entrepreneurial world.

Let's start talking about ways you can generate an income! Here's a few initial thoughts to remember:

1) You gotta make it fun! If it's not fun for you, you will not be passionate about what you are doing.

2) The Three 'P's are a must! Passion, Perseverance and Persistence.

3) Every *little* thing you do MATTERS!

4) Do not let anyone steal your dreams!

5) Put yourself OUT THERE… take risks.

6) Do not let fear stop you. Be afraid, but do it anyway. You only fail if you don't try.

7) DON'T JUDGE YOUR INSIDES BY SOMEBODY ELSE'S OUTSIDE!!! (You heard this before-it's worth repeating)

8) Never, ever, ever give up!

Note: email me at Patti@teenscashcoach.com for the PDF of this chapter, so you can complete these forms easily! I will email it to you!

Let's get started!

What do you LOVE to do?

Let's start thinking about what type of business you want to start. Ideally, you are doing something you love to do, while making money. Let's utilize your talents and skills!

List what you love to do here:

_____
_____
_____
_____
_____
_____
_____
_____

Here are some talents and skills in which I excel: (what do people say you are good at?)

_____

_____

_____

_____

_____

Write down any business ideas that you think you'd like to do. For now, just write everything that comes to your mind and do not judge. Do not eliminate anything, you can do that later. Be open to crazy ideas! Let your imagination go!!

_____

_____

_____

_____

_____

What is your 'WHY'? Why do you want to start a business? Is it purely for financial gain? Want to buy a car? Do you want to make a difference in the world somehow? Do you want a peaceful financial future? Understanding your 'why' is important for several reasons. It will help you stay on track when you get frustrated (which you will at some point), it will help prioritize your 'to-do' list and it will keep you motivated and inspired.

What is your why?

_____

_____

_____

_____

_____

P.S. Once you have written your WHY, I want you to read it daily. Post it on your bathroom mirror; keep a copy in your wallet or purse and maybe one copy near your bed. Refer back to it, as this will keep you motivated, especially on those days you feel overwhelmed.

Basic Business Models For Teens

Service: You do some type of service work

Sell product: You sell a product that you have made or produced yourself.

Sell other people's products: You are selling a product that someone else has produced or made.

A Service based business is one of the best businesses to start out with. Why?

It usually does not cost you much money (if anything), yet it can be very financially rewarding. With your service, your client must BENEFIT somehow! You always need to ADD VALUE.

Either by:

1. Saving your client **money** by using your service
2. Saving your client their **valuable time** by using your service
3. **Taking away** some type of **pain** they experience by using your service.

Here are some business ideas if you are having a tough time thinking of one! With all businesses, always ask for referrals and testimonials. Be sure to include these testimonials on your flyers and website! As always, get permission from your parents to do any of these jobs!

Babysitting: Don't just baby-sit! Take a CPR and first aid class. Bring books to read and toys to play with for the kids. Have testimonials (referrals) from other clients and give those to your prospects.

Dog walking: add dog brushing for added income. Take doggie bones as a gift, which will WOW your client. Great help for the elderly, disabled individuals or busy parents!

Weeding/raking leaves: eliminate the gardener and show your client how you can save them money. Offer to come in once a week to maintain their garden and earn extra income.

Mowing lawn:- Again, you are saving gardener fees. You can charge the client for both services separately and earn extra $$. This is generally a higher liability, as it can be dangerous. Be sure you know how to use a lawnmower properly and are extra careful when doing this! Have your parents show you the correct and safe way to handle this machinery.

Car washing and/or car detailing:- Save your client the cost and time of going to a car wash. When you do a good job, you will potentially be able to do this on regular basis (maybe weekly) for a steady income. Get referrals as the neighbors watch you every week!

Washing windows:- Windows get dirty and for the right price, you will find work! You would need to do single story homes, if doing the inside and outside, but can do two story homes if cleaning the inside windows only.

Running errands if you have a car:- If you have a car and a good driving record, this can be a huge timesaver for many busy parents. You can charge by the hour, the mileage or both. Make sure you ask your parents about your car insurance on this one!

Nanny for mom entrepreneur/executives who work at home-With many people working from home these days, juggling kids and work can get tricky. Charge by the hour and get paid for watching their kids while these busy executives can get their job done.

Office assistant: for work- at- home parents. Save your clients valuable time by doing some simple filing, answering phone or organizing their offices. This is a much-needed service!

Mistletoe bags:-This is seasonal, but easy and fun money! Get some mistletoe, place in pretty plastic bags and throw a ribbon around it. Charge a few bucks and sell away!!

Cleaning homes:-This can be a great cost saver for your clients. Housekeepers are expensive and you can save clients serious $$. You can do simple work, like vacuuming and dusting, or the full home, which does include bathrooms.

Taking out/in trash cans:- Seems simple enough, but people are busy and forgetful. Charge a simple $10/month fee to take out and bring in trashcans. It takes less than 2 minutes to do, yet can help your client tremendously. If you can get several clients on one street, this can be especially cool (and profitable)! This is especially good for the elderly or physically disabled.

Selling other people's products:- This is a bit trickier and better suited for the older teen. You may need to look into a resale license and collecting sales tax. A resale license enables you to purchase items without paying sales tax. (You'll need your parents help with this one, especially if you're under 18)

Selling items on Ebay:- You can sell items on eBay that you have made (produced) or items that you have purchased from somebody else. Many people buy at swap meets, flea markets or discount stores and then sell these items on eBay.

Helping with preparing meals:- For those of you who love to cook, you can save your clients valuable time by cooking for them. This is another wonderful service for the elderly or disabled.

Social media marketing consultant:- If you are savvy with the social media madness going on these days, many small business owners would love to hire you! Facebook, twitter, Instagram, Pinterest, YouTube and LinkedIn are all valuable tools for businesses, but many business owners do not understand how to use these properly. Rescue them with your knowledge and get paid nicely for it!

Graphic designer for websites:- If your talent lies in creativity and you have computer skills, helping a small business owner with graphic design might be a great choice. This is oftentimes a costly expense for a business, so you can save your client big money.

Help senior citizens understand the computer:- What is easy to you, is complete babble for many, especially senior citizens! Spend some time teaching simple internet strategies, such as surfing the net, getting and sending emails with attachments or showing them how to copy/paste a word document.

Tutor your strongest subject:- Many students struggle with different subjects and oftentimes learn better from one of their 'peeps'. Share your strength in a particular subject and earn a nice income. This is a money saver for parents, as traditional tutors can be expensive. (I personally tutored Calculus in college and made great money!)

Garage sales:- Like they say, one man's trash is another man's treasure. Find some goodies that you just won't use again and sell them. This is more of a one-time sale, but worth considering for quick cash.

Love photography?-Sell your digital photos!: Many sites will pay you money for your pictures. Check out shutterstock.com, 123RF.com, dreamstime.com, crestock.com and fotolia.com. There are many more, but check those to start!

Pet sitting:- When people travel, they oftentimes have to board their dogs or cats. Show them how you can save them money and give their dog individual attention by pet sitting. Teach them a new trick for added fun and customer satisfaction! (The dog, not the pet owner ☺)

Can you sing or play an instrument?:-Do what you do best and have fun, while earning money. Sing or play music at weddings, birthdays or any other special occasion. Great for someone on a budget, who cannot quite afford paying a professional performer.

Teach music lessons:- Formal music lessons can be expensive, yet many parents want their child to know how to play an instrument. If you have the musical bug, share your talents and earn some fun, easy money.

Recycle cans or plastic bottles:- This super easy habit of recycling can help fill your pockets with cash quickly. Volunteer to help your neighbors recycle too. Plus, you are helping the environment.

Blogging:- This online business venture is not quick cash, but can work great over time. After you have built up your 'followers', you can begin to sell or refer products for commissions-this is called becoming an *affiliate*. You can also earn money by doing product reviews or advertising on your site. Find something you love writing about and blog away!

Enjoy writing?: If you have a talent for writing, consider writing for others. Check out www.elance.com to learn how to get started. You can also write articles and submit to magazines, both offline and online.

Sell your used books:- If you have books that you are not going to use again, consider selling them. It is not a regular income, but a source of quick cash if needed.

Clean out refrigerators:-I may personally hire you for this one! You can offer this as an added service for those people you help house clean or dog walk. Charge a flat fee, rather than hourly. You do not want to rush through it, yet you do not want to appear going slowly for more money.

Bookkeeping:- If you're good with numbers, helping a small business owner manage their books is great source of income, not to mention experience for your resume. Your responsibilities may be as basic as paying bills online to creating their financial statements every month.

Sports Coach:- Do you excel at a particular sport? Be a private coach for a fraction of the cost, while loving what you do!

YouTube videos: There are many teens making a killing creating YouTube videos. Your success will take time, as you build up your follower base, but once you have a following, you can make some great money. Gaming is especially popular, as are fun, entertaining daily vlogs. (Video blogs) Be sure to check with your parents before you put anything online.

Remember, one client can mean several sources of income. For example, once you prove your good work ethic and value in doing one service, clients will oftentimes hire you for another. The same client that you do gardening for would be a good candidate for teaching computer skills and cleaning out their refrigerator.

Again, be sure to get client testimonials and add to your website or flyer. Every experience you have will give you tools for the next job and look great on your resume.

You Need A Business Plan

Next step, you need a business and marketing plan. Depending upon your business, this can be very simple and basic, or a bit more complicated and detailed. I will cover some basics, but there are many great resources online. Just google "business plan" and you will find many templates and resources. Don't let this part scare you and please do not avoid it. If you fail to plan, you plan to fail!

Here is a basic list, but remember, some of these may not apply to you at this point. I am listing some items that you should consider much later, as your business grows, so refer to this as needed. Again, most of the businesses mentioned above do not need a business plan. This list is more of a reference for later.

- Prepare a business plan
- Prepare financial forecasts- How much money will you need?
- Find lawyer, accountant and insurance agent (not likely needed at this point)
- Get a P.O. Box or 'mailbox' address (do not use home address)
- Open bank account in business name
- Decide on entity structure (LLC, Corporation etc.) (Again, not likely needed at this point)
- Apply for DBA (Doing Business As)
- Apply for business license (if applicable)
- Design logo
- Create marketing campaign/marketing material

- Design and purchase business cards
- Design and purchase stationary
- Develop introduction letter
- Design flyers
- Develop database of prospects (offline and online)
- Set up home office, if working from home.
- Buy office supplies
- Build and develop website
- Find a mentor or coach
- Join networking group/mastermind
- Build relationships!
- Have fun! ☺

Why do we need a Business Plan?

When you are planning a vacation, what is the first thing you do?

Probably decide on the destination! Once you know where you want to go (your vacation spot), and where you are starting from (your home), you would probably pull out a map, maybe GPS or go to mapquest.com, right? Are you going to drive or fly? Who is going with you? Got cash for gas and food? Are you staying in a hotel?

I admit, it's the boring part, but it must be done!!

You need to do the same thing when putting a business together. You must know the:

- **Who**—Who is involved in your business? Are you in business by yourself or do you have partners? Who are your customers?

- **When**—Timelines of goals… 1st year goals, 2nd year etc.

- **What**—What are you selling— products or services or both?

- **Where**—Where do you plan on marketing? Worldwide (online) or your neighborhood?

- **How**—How do you plan on marketing? How much money (capital) do you need?

- **Why**—Why are you doing this business? What is your mission statement?

Time for YOUR business plan!

Name of business_____

First section: Explain your business.

Pretend you're writing a cover letter to your ideal client. (This is usually done last)

_____
_____
_____
_____
_____
_____
_____
_____
_____
_____
_____

Second section: What are your goals for your company?

In bullet format, describe your objectives and goals for the next few years. How much money do you plan to make? Where do you want to make an impact?

- _____
- _____
- _____
- _____
- _____

Third section: What is your mission statement?

Tell others what *benefits* they will experience by doing business with you. (This mission statement should be on every piece of marketing material...flyers, website, business cards etc.)

_____

_____

_____

_____

_____

Fourth section: Company summary- how will your business operate?

How will your product or service be rendered? What specifically is your product or service? Describe the features and benefits of your product or service.

_____

_____

_____

_____

_____

_____

Fifth section: Market analysis- who is your competition?

How do you differ from them? What makes you better?

How much does your product or service cost the client?

_____

_____

_____

_____

Sixth Section: Marketing-

Describe your ideal client (your target market) in detail. Age, gender, income level, education, what car drive, what type of neighborhood do they live in. Be specific. How do you plan on marketing to them? Offline or online? I suggest both. (We will cover this later)

_____

_____

_____

_____

_____

_____

_____

_____

Seventh Section: Capital!

How much money do you need to get started? Where are you planning to get that money? Borrow from parents? Chores? Another job? You need to show others (someday, possibly a bank) how you plan to repay them. Example: You borrow $200 from parents to print flyers, biz cards, website, and purchase items to get started. You charge $15 per hour for your services. $200/$15 = 13.3 hours- So you need 13 hours of work to break even and pay your parents back. If you work only 3 hours per week, you can pay them back in approximately 4-5 weeks. Nice!

_____

_____

_____

_____

_____

_____

_____

Let's talk Marketing!!

Marketing is crucial to your success. You can be the absolute BEST at what you do, but if nobody knows about you, or how to find you, you will not have a successful business!

You must share your product and service with your target market in a way that touches them. As we mentioned earlier, you need to fill a need, save them money, make them money or take away a pain.

Remember to ask yourself these important questions: Who is your target market? Where will you find them?

Let's start online:

People will do business with people they know, like and trust. These online marketing techniques will do just that! Be authentic and genuine. Nobody likes a fake!

Social media is huge and FREE!

Join Facebook, Instagram, Pinterest, Twitter and LinkedIn. Go where your target market hangs out. (Be sure to get the okay from your parents to join these sites.) Do posts and updates regularly to meet people. (I'm going to assume you are already very active on most of these sites)

Go to online forums or blogs that your target market would visit. Post comments and refer back to your website. Be engaging, add value and be authentic. (Also a FREE way to reach your market)

Video is BIG! Post videos on YouTube of your products and services, or how your products and services are helping others. If you are a musician giving lessons, strut your stuff and post it! Post this video on your website as well. (Another FREEBIE...can you tell I love free☺) Cross post this video on your social media sites. Share a tip or tool, again, always bring value.

Find people that market to the same target audience, but are not competitors, and cross promote each other. If you are a tutor, find a person that markets to parents of teens and promote each other's services. (Partner with a company that sells sport products. Maybe their teens do sports and need certain grades to stay on the team.)

Offer a FREEBIE on your website-This strategy is awesome and used by some of the best marketers. On your website, offer something for free. In order for people to have access to this free item, they will need to put in their name and email address. You now can start an email campaign and email them on a regular basis. Don't email them junk or sales pitches every week! You have to deliver value and good content. You can then sprinkle in information about your products or services every month or so. Don't oversell! They will opt-out of your email blasts and you will lose them forever.

This will cost you a little, as the program to do mass email blasts will charge you a monthly fee. A few great resources are www.constantcontact.com, www.mailchimp.com, www.aweber.com and www.1shoppingcart.com.

Look at my website as an example, www.teenscashcoach.com.

Be sure to protect your intellectual property by obtaining a copyright, trademark or patent. If you write something, use the © symbol and date. A great resource for this **is** www.legalzoom.com. Be sure to explore your options. Example:

Teens Cash Coach Copyright © 2010 All Rights Reserved

I have actually trademarked "Teens Cash Coach", so if you have a company name you want to protect, be sure to do this.

Let's go Offline

There are many ways to promote offline, but most cost money. In today's digital world, there is less and less of print media, so I would not necessarily suggest these, especially as you are starting out. Down the road, some of these may make sense for you. A few examples are:

- Flyers/brochures: place where your target market hangs out.
- Advertising- local paper or trade magazine
- Writing articles for exposure, not payment. Writing for other blogs is great.
- Direct mailings (cost of brochure or postcard plus postage can be expensive)

Here are some that cost little, or no, money:
- Press releases- submit to newspapers, local and/or statewide.
- Networking groups- meet people!
- Mastermind groups- Great minds think alike
- Speaking engagements (You're the speaker for exposure)
- Chamber of Commerce meetings

There are many other outlets to consider, both offline and online, as it seems every day there is a new site or app being launched. Talk with others, especially a mentor and explore your options.

You can order business cards at www.vistaprint.com free. They will charge you a nominal fee for shipping and handling. This should be considered part of your 'start up' costs that was discussed with the business plan.

There are many styles and colors to choose from. If you want to import your own pictures or art, they will charge you an additional fee, but this is not necessary to start. They have many themes to choose from. I'm sure you can find one that will work for you.

Having a website is a must if you plan to build a longer-term business. It does lend itself as a 'billboard' for yourself, but you can certainly start earning money without one.

If you have an online business, this of course, is a different story. Most of what we discussed here relates to a service type business that is not online. As your business grows, having an online presence is highly recommended.

You can also set up a blog, which is a great way to keep your site constantly changing. A typical website is 'static' meaning the information does not change very often. With a blog, you can update easily, whenever you want. I would highly suggest you set up a blog versus a static website. They are much less expensive and much simpler to navigate. WordPress blogs are super easy. Hosting your website normally costs extra, but not terribly expensive.

If you prefer to purchase your own domain and host separately, you may do that. I have found that www.godaddy.com is a great place to purchase a domain and www.bluehost.com is a great place for hosting. You should shop and compare for yourself, but these are two sites I personally use. Bluehost will have specials, so talk to someone live and negotiate the price.

I also recommend you purchase your name as a domain. I have www.PattiHandy.com, which hosts my mortgage business. I will keep that domain as long as I am working, regardless of what I am doing.

As you grow into various businesses, (most entrepreneurs have several businesses) you can always navigate your followers back to your name site.

In the end, make sure you enjoy what you are doing, giving value to your customers and utilizing that brilliant mind of yours!

Remember: email me at Patti@teenscashcoach.com for the PDF of this chapter, so you can complete these forms easily, without having to write in the book! I will email it to you!

The **Action Items** for this chapter is to complete all the sections above!

7

The Secret Sauce to Spending Wisely

"It's not how far you fall, but how high you bounce that counts."

Zig Ziglar

In researching the profiles of affluent people, I have discovered there are some common belief systems and habits, especially when it comes to money.

First, they live well below their means. What exactly does this mean? What does this suggest for you?

It suggests you do not spend your money on the latest gadget that you feel you absolutely have to have, when in reality you do not need it at all. It means you don' t need to buy the latest pair of jeans that everyone loves, especially when they cost $200. Stop trying to impress people with things.

Do yourself a huge favor - before you buy something, ask yourself, "Is this purchase more important than my future financial freedom day?" Wealthy people realize that their financial independence is more important than what people think of them. They realize their social status is second fiddle to their wealth and financial peace.

I understand there is a delicate balance between enjoying your life today and preparing for tomorrow. After all, having millions when you retire will not be exciting if you spent your entire life hoarding your cash.

It's very important that you enjoy the journey of your life and treat yourself to those things you deserve. Just remember you also deserve to enjoy a peaceful life, not worrying about money, with the ease of paying your bills and giving back. It does take discipline. It means creating healthy lifestyle habits, and it means making the right spending decisions. And, yes, it does suggest there will be some sacrifices.

I also understand the peer pressure with which you are faced. I was young once myself. The ironic thing is that some of that peer pressure follows you to adulthood, which is why there are so many people today struggling financially. So, the sooner you learn how to deal with peer pressure, the better off you will be in dealing with it as an adult.

It comes back to what I mentioned earlier: wealthy people realize that their financial peace is more important than other people's opinions. Seriously, is someone else's opinion more important than yours? Especially when it comes to you, your family, your future, and your quality of life?

So, how do you balance this? I do have some suggestions that will put you on the path to spending wisely.

Track, track, track

First, track your spending. How? It's simple! Write down everything you spend during the day—not forever, just for a few weeks, maybe a month. Or enter it on an app or on your phone in a note.

What this does is create a healthy habit of being aware of what and where you spend your money. Maybe it will make you think twice as well. At the end of the month, add up all those expenditures you made. Maybe it was a coffee, juice, or fast food that you could have grabbed at home. This is the money that you could have saved and not really felt in your day-to-day activities. Eating out is one of the worst ways to "eat" away your money.

Again, you have to balance enjoying life with planning for your future. I am not suggesting you never eat out; just watch the little expenditures that you may not think make a big difference. In reality, those dollars add up to big dollars over time. This is a separate step from your checkbook register and balancing your checkbook. (We will cover that more in detail later.)

Watch the impulse buying. When you see something you want, ask yourself, "Is this item a want or a need?" If it's a need, make sure you can pay for it in cash, not by borrowing (credit). Have you met your savings goal for the week? If it's a want, ask yourself why you want it.

Is it to impress your friends? Is it something you think is cool? Wait three days and think about it to decide if you really want it. Often, you'll realize you do not want it or you would rather spend that money on something else you really want. If you still want it, make sure it comes out of your play money and not your savings. Have you shopped around for the best price?

Being aware of this will teach you to be responsible and to respect your money. Impulse buying will put you into debt, which will create unhealthy spending habits, as you grow older. Credit card debt is very expensive and can take years to resolve. Remember, borrowing money from your parents or friends is considered debt too.

I recommend you keep a spending tracker. As I mentioned, make notes in your cell or use an app, but note the items below which you should include.

Daily Spending Tracker

Date	What Bought	How Much $$	Why Did I Buy

It's that simple. As I mentioned earlier, keep this list for a few weeks, possibly a month. This will build your awareness and lifestyle habit of healthy spending. Remember; always ask yourself if the purchase is a *want* or a *need*. Creating this habit now will pay off big time as you grow and start living your life as an adult. Frankly, these same habits should continue forever.

The Monthly Spending Tracker

I do not like the word budget, but I like what the word represents. Let me explain. A budget is like a diet to me. Nobody likes to diet because it implies we need to give something up. Well, we do. We give up the *temporary joy* we experience when we eat something yummy that may not be good for us.

The rewards and benefits far outweigh what we give up. When we diet, we do so to become healthier, more energized and live a longer, better quality life. We are fit, and we feel better about ourselves, too.

So, what's more important?

A temporary treat or lifelong health? Same goes for your money. Your budget ("spending plan" is my preferred term) is about watching what you spend and having a plan to secure a better, healthier future. Please keep in mind that I'm not saying to live this strict life of only healthy eating and only frugal spending. Life is too short for that. Moderation is key. The goal is *overall good habits* and lifestyle choices.

So, how do we tie all this together? You need to organize your financial commitments and stick to a plan. To help you do this, I put a monthly tracker chart together for you. This plan is assuming you still live at home, without the expense of rent/mortgage and the other expenses that go along with being in your own home (utilities, taxes, homeowner's insurance, etc.)

This tracker (plan) will help you stick with your obligations, put aside money for investing, and keep you on track. It will help you allocate your money and learn to manage it properly. Here's an example: You just got a paycheck for $500, and you're thinking, "*whoop whoop, let's go shopping.*"

Stop that brain freeze and realize you have financial obligations first. Once you review this tracker, you can determine what you have left over after your commitments are taken care of.

In the chapter on saving, I will cover in detail the percentages that should go to savings vs. spending. This will help you determine where your money goes as well. All this information will tie together.

Monthly Spending Tracker

Where oh where has all the money gone?
(For those that still live at home)

Income:	
Wages/ Salary	
Allowance	
Other	
Expenses	
Savings	
Car Payment	
Car Insurance	
Gas-car	
Car Maintenance	
Public Transportation	
Cell Phone	
Entertainment	
CD/DVD's	
Subscriptions	
Clothing	
Hair/Nails	
Gym/Health Club	
Textbooks	
School Supplies	
Credit Card	
Gifts	
Donations	
Food/Drinks	
Other	

Now, Writing Out The Check

I realize that writing a check is becoming a thing of the past, as most of us use debit cards these days. Having said that, it's still important to know how to use a check, balance your checkbook and manage your checking account.

Even when you use your debit card, you should be documenting all those expenditures, and deposits to maintain a running balance. Otherwise, you run the risk of an overdraft fee. The fundamentals are the same, whether you write a check or use your debit card.

I'm showing this process to you so understand the concept of balancing your checkbook, tracking spending, keeping a running balance and watching your account. With the increase of identity theft issues, it's important you check your accounts several times a week. You should know your balances, within a few dollars, at all times.

I'm sure you have seen a check before, but here is a picture for illustration purposes. The steps below may seem very simplistic, and they are, but I want to walk you through even the most basic of steps.

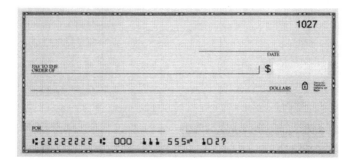

Here are the specific items to enter and how it is done:

The **date** is the current date. You can either write out the month or just use the number. For example, you can write, January 27, 2017 or 1/27/2017. Either way is fine.

Pay to the order of: The person or company that the check is payable to. Make sure to fill out completely. Don't leave this spot blank or let someone else fill out. If you are at an establishment that has a stamp, you can have them stamp it. I suggest you watch them stamp it to confirm.

Amount $: This is where you put the amount: dollars and cents in number format. For example, $25.40.

Dollars line: The long line under the "pay to the order" line is where you write out the dollar amount you put in the amount box. For example, with the amount above, it would read, "Twenty-five dollars and 40/100————." Always draw a line across to the end.

Signature: This is where you sign your name and promise to pay.

Memo/For: This is an optional section for you to fill out. It allows you to make note of what the purchase was for, in case you want to reference it later.

There you go! You're on your way. Remember, just because you have checks, does not mean you have the money to use those checks. Balance your checkbook every month and keep a running tally on your balance always. If you use your debit card, make sure to note where and what you spent.

The checkbook register

So, here's the beautiful thing. Now that you are in the habit of thinking before you spend and documenting your spending, the checkbook register becomes very easy. It's a natural progression and a continuation of what you have already been doing—with a couple, easy additions.

Once you are old enough to open a checking account, you're given a book of checks along with a checkbook register. This register is much like the daily tracker you are already using-hopefully.

It's meant to help you know the current balance in your checking account. Every deposit and every withdrawal is written down, so that at any moment, you know what available balance you have. Failure to do this can be expensive. Let me explain.

Having a checking account is a huge responsibility, and it can cost you dearly if you do not maintain (balance) it every month. If you happen to spend more than what you have, the banks will charge you a fee that will hurt. It can be in the form of an overdraft or service fee. Paying these fees is no different from you taking a $20 bill and lighting it on fire. Poof, it's gone. Think about how hard you worked for that money and don't let that happen.

When you use a debit card, it's the same as writing a check. The expense is deducted from your account immediately and you must write this expenditure down in your checkbook register. A debit card looks like a credit card, but is very different. Debit cards are like cash - remember, once you use your debit card, the funds are withdrawn from your bank account immediately.

Some banks may also charge you a monthly service fee, phone bank fees, ATM fees, or overdraft protection fees. Be sure to deduct these fees in your checkbook register, as these can add up and mess up your math. Most banks or credit unions have accounts specifically for teens that will waive these fees. Be sure to shop around. You should not be paying these fees.

So, let's talk about balancing your checkbook. Here is the step-by-step process.

First, let me say, it is not that bad. If you keep up with it monthly, it is quite easy. You must do this every month to confirm that neither you nor the bank made an error. (Yes, banks can make errors, too). If you do not check and balance, it can result in an overdrawn account and expensive bank charges. As I said earlier, you work too hard to let the bank take that money away from you.

Okay, let's start!

Step 1:

Take your checkbook register, bank statement, and put them side by side. Go down each check that you wrote (or debit card purchase) and compare that to your bank statement. Put a check by each entry that exists on both the statement and your checkbook register. This means that your check "cleared" the bank. Do the same for all of your deposits. Remember to add interest earned and deduct service charges from your checkbook register. These will appear on your statement.

Now, Step 2 will help you compare the two by just adding and subtracting. The most common mistakes are arithmetic, so use a calculator to help.

Step 2:

On your bank statement do the following:

Start with: Ending balance from statement	$
Add: Deposits not on statement	$
Subtotal =	$
Subtract: Checks outstanding (did not clear)	$
BALANCE (this should agree with checkbook)	$

In your checkbook register do the following:

Start with: Balance from checkbook	$
Add: Interest earned or other credit shown on statement, but not in checkbook	$
Subtotal =	$
Subtract: Service charges or other debits shown on statement, but not in checkbook	$
BALANCE (this should agree with statement)	$

Step 3:

Be very proud of yourself! This is a huge step towards being responsible and managing your money.

Having said all this about checkbook registers and balancing your checkbook, you do have an alternative. Banking online and various accounting software has made the task of paying bills and balancing your checkbook much easier. Understanding the concepts of maintaining your balances and tracking your spending is still imperative. (This is why I took you through the exercise.) If you decide to bank online and use checks concurrently, be sure to keep your checkbook register updated.

Your lifestyle choices

So, you have learned how to track your spending and balance your checkbook. Awesome! I touched on the topic of lifestyle choices and not being concerned with other's opinions, but I want to go a bit deeper on this subject.

I know you will be working hard for your money. (I'm confident you will also be working smart for your money). It is so important to enjoy the journey of life, embrace the moments with your family and friends, travel, enjoy a hobby, and just do what makes you happy. It's not all about working and saving. Life is precious and life is short, so I encourage you to take it all in with an open heart.

As I mentioned earlier, it takes a delicate balance of wisdom to enjoy your life, while planning for your future. Without a plan in place, your dreams of financial freedom and financial peace simply will not happen. Keep in mind, I'm not just referring to retirement. Financial freedom happens throughout your life.

I would love to see you enjoy life to its fullest, realize your goals and dreams, and live life with no regrets. You are the only one that can make that happen and the only one that has your dream.

Having said all that, here is the point that I started with. Your lifestyle choices and habits will greatly affect you realizing your dreams. Here it is in simple terms: Imagine you are out with your friends, and you stop for lunch, juice or a coffee. Let's say that stop costs $4. Harmless enough, right? Wrong. Did you know that if you put $4 a day into an account that earns 10% on average, you would have almost $17,000 in just ten years?

Let's say you do that same $4 a day for 20 years. Well, the magic of compounding interest and time would bring that to almost $61,000. Shocking isn't it?

It's those little choices that you make day to day that add up to big differences in your life. Whether it is a fast-food stop or an impulse purchase, these choices will impact your bottom line faster than you can say, "Mom, can I borrow some money?"

Please understand that I am not saying you can't ever enjoy a nice meal out with your friends. By all means, go enjoy yourself. Just do it in moderation, just like that diet we spoke of earlier. Don't splurge, because you know what comes next. Although it goes without saying, always use cash (and track, of course) these outings. Do not put on a credit card.

Some last thoughts regarding spending: As in life, when things are *in order,* meaning organized, there is a tendency to experience more harmony and peace. When there is chaos, there is almost always some type of headache and/or heartache. When it comes to your spending, keep all receipts and bills in an organized file. Know where everything is in case you need it for tax purposes, school purposes, or anything else. Getting in the habit of staying organized will serve you very well as you get older.

This will teach you to stay on top of your paperwork, whether it relates to your personal life or work life. As you get older, you'll need to organize your home receipts, investment statements, real estate documentation, insurance information, living trust (getting ahead of myself here—sorry), and much more. I realize that most of this does not pertain to you right now, but it will before you know it.

So, enjoy life, spend your money, but do it wisely. Watch the impulse buying, watch the fast food outings, and don't fret about the latest and greatest gizmo to impress your friends. Have fun, but keep your financial freedom destination in mind, too.

Action Items

What are the top five things you spend money on every week?

_____

_____

_____

_____

_____

Describe the peer pressure you feel.

_____

_____

_____

_____

_____

When you spend money, what emotions are you feeling?

Joy Sadness Acceptance   Anticipation

Stress   Fear   Anger   Surprise

Excitement Disappointment Happiness

What did you buy today? How about yesterday? This past week?

_____

_____

_____

Now, go back and circle the purchases you are still happy about that fulfilled needs. Cross out the purchases that you regret, the ones that were 'wants' or impulse purchases.

What does your financial independence day look like? Do you own your own car? House? A certain amount of money in the bank? Describe in detail.

What are your savings goals for the week?

Write down three things that you will commit to that will start your journey to financial independence.

How do you typically pay for your purchases, cash or credit card? Why?

_____

_____

_____

After using the spending tracker, what are you typically finding you spend money on? Food? Coffee? Entertainment? Downloads?

_____

_____

_____

_____

What is your gross monthly income? Either from a job, chores or any other source.

_____

What is your monthly net income? Source?

_____

_____

List five places that you regularly shop, as well as five stores that you could comparison shop.

_____

_____

_____

_____

Has the spending tracker helped you determine where you
can cut back? Explain.

_____

_____

_____

_____

_____

How much money can you commit to putting in long term
and short term savings every month?

_____

8

To Save or Not to Save

"Only those who dare to fail greatly can ever achieve greatly."

Robert F. Kennedy

 How many times have you heard about an athlete or actor that has made millions, yet ended up broke? Can you imagine making $20 million a year as an athlete or per movie, yet having nothing in savings? Unfortunately, it happens.

Why does this happen? How does this happen?

In my opinion, it's a lack of savings discipline and out of control spending. Money management habits are not in place and one day they wake up and realize they are in deep trouble.

Saving money is somewhat like an art. It requires discipline, focus, determination and a deep desire to create something. What are you creating with savings? Peace of mind. Financial freedom. The ability to make a difference in the world by giving back.

Learning how to save money can come easily for some, yet for others it can prove to be difficult. It comes down to a few basic steps: Let's first take a look at what saving is- simply put, take the money you have coming in (income) and subtract the money you have going out (expenses). The difference is savings.

This may seem simplistic and pretty obvious. And it is, but keep in mind this simple fact- *to increase your savings you need to either make more money, or spend less.*

Plain and simple.

One of your "expenses" should be "savings." In fact, you should pay yourself first, every single month. More on this later.

Increasing income can happen in various ways, depending upon your age. If you have a job, ask yourself, "Can I do better by working somewhere else?" "Is this company paying me what I am worth?" "What are my options for higher paying jobs?" Better yet, ask yourself, "How can I take what I love to do, utilize my skills and talents, and create my own income?" You may need to start your own company while working a regular job to keep the money coming in. (As you know from a previous chapter, I love the idea of entrepreneurship.)

Decreasing expenses—this is where you will need to take a hard look at things. In the spending chapter, I gave you a spending tracker. If used, this will shed some light on where all your money is going. I suggest you look hard at this list and determine where you can shave off some expenses. How much are you eating out? Coffees? Downloading songs? Remember, every dollar counts! You get the idea.

It comes down to lifestyle habits, and sometimes a lifestyle change has to be made. Your priorities have to be crystal clear. Is your first car or first home more important than eating out? As I have said earlier, this is not about cutting out fun or enjoyment out of life. It's about creating healthy habits and an awareness and a desire for financial independence. Some things just have to be eliminated, at least for now.

Think about the shift from 'instant gratification' to 'delayed gratification.' It is hard, I get it. All I ask is you become aware of this.

It's about balancing. Keep this in mind: as you create these healthy habits at a young age, you will be setting yourself up for an amazing future—one filled with financial peace and abundance. You can dine anywhere you desire and treat your friends if you want. As I just mentioned, it is about delayed gratification. *Realize that you may have to give up something today to have something so much better tomorrow.*

Paying yourself first!

One expense that should be number one on your list is paying you. That's right. The first payment you make every month is to a savings or investment account in your name. I don't care if its $10, $50, $100 or more a month; just make it. Get in the habit of paying yourself first, every single month, consistently. You will be shocked at how quickly this adds up.

I would recommend you have the amount automatically deducted from your checking account and transferred to the savings or investment account you opened for this purpose. Most banks will have this automatic withdrawal feature for you; all you need to do is fill out a form at your bank, or sign up for it online. If this is done automatically, you're less likely to forget, or worse, spend the money on something else.

This one simple behavior is something wealthy individuals do. They understand the power of compounding interest and the power of time. They also live well below their means, as I mentioned earlier. This savings habit is a priority for them. There is no magic bullet or overnight wealth.

Compounding interest and time: your new best friends!

This is the part where I have some fun. I'm always excited to see people's faces when I give them hard numbers when it comes to saving money over time. I get everything from shock to laughter. I like them both.

Let's assume you've opened up a savings or investment account with $100 to start. You can manage to put an additional $40 per month into the account. That's $10 a week. No biggie. You probably wouldn't miss it.

If that account was earning 8% interest, compounded annually, your account balance after five years would be— drum roll please— $3,188.18. Amazing huh? Just $40 a month and a few years later, you have over three thousand bucks.

Now, to show you how the power of time and compound interest work, take that same example just a step further. What if you put that same $40 a month into the same 8% account, only this time left it there for ten years, instead of five years?

Another drum roll please—$7,725.73! How about twenty years, just for fun—$24,189. What about forty years? $136,467! Do you see the power of compounding?

Think about this- how much of that money is principal and how much is interest? Let's do the math. Using the example of twenty years, you have put in $9,700 of your own money ($100 initial deposit plus $40/month x 240 months). If you have $24,189 that would mean $14,489 is pure interest.

What about the forty-year example? Your own deposits would total $19,300 ($100 initial deposit plus $40/month x 480 months). Yet, you would have $136,467, which means that $117,167 is pure interest. Can you say "free money"?

Let's step it up a bit

Imagine if you could put more than $40 a month away. Let's say you've managed to cut some expenses out and were able to increase that monthly savings number to $100. Assuming the same scenario, starting with a $100 deposit, 8% interest compounded annually you would see this:

After 5 years	$7,750
After 10 years	$18,990
After 20 years	$59,773
After 40 years	$337,909

Here's the most important point I want you to take from this section. **Start early!**

Want to retire a millionaire? Check out this example!

For this example, I am going to share a story of two friends. Let's call them Rich and Les.

Rich understands how compound interest works and he decides to start saving money early, because he wants to retire comfortably. At age 19, he starts to put $3,000 per year into an account (do not freak, it is just over $8.00 a day). He does this every year, for 8 years, and then he stops. Essentially, he has put $24,000 of his own money at this point. He does not add any more of his own funds to this account.

Care to take a wild guess as to how much money he has at age 60? Remember, he only deposited money for 8 years, for a total of $24,000. The remaining years, the money just grew, with the beauty of compounding.

At age 60, he has $964,129!!! That is almost a million bucks!!

All this on his $24,000, because he started early!!! Crazy amazing, isn't it?

Now, let's talk about Les. He decided to put money into a new car, enjoyed life out with friends and never saved. At age 27, he figured he better start saving for the future and stop playing so hard. So, he decided to put the same $3,000 into an account, just like Rich.

This scenario turns out much different.

Because Les started just a few years later, he didn't have the luxury of stopping after 8 years, assuming he wanted to retire with close to a million dollars. He had to save $3,000 per year for the remaining 34 years!

This works out to $102,000 of his hard-earned money, as opposed to the $24,000 that Rich saved. And, here's the kicker....

At age 60, Les had a total of $810,073. Not a bad nest egg, but this is less than what Rich had, even after he had to save for many more years and deposited more of his own money!

This is a great example of the power of compounding interest and why I encourage you to start early! I realize I have said this a few times, but now you understand why!

Both of the above examples assume a 10% average return over the time invested, in a tax deferred retirement account.

Search online and you will find many great sites that will allow you to play with different financial calculators.

Let's talk about your dreams and goals

It is so important to have dreams and goals for yourself. It fuels the soul with inspiration and determination. Having something that touches your heart and mind, whatever it is, will stir up feelings of hope, excitement and passion. We, as human beings, need this.

So, what does this have to do with money? Well, most dreams and goals have something to do with money, in one way or another. It might be to make a certain income to provide for your family, it might be to give a certain amount every year to a charity that touches your heart, or it may be to start a business venture that you have always wanted. Whatever those dreams, having good spending and savings habits will be an integral part of whether you reach those goals or not.

Learning how to save early, having the discipline necessary to consistently save, and understanding the importance of savings early will prove to be a necessary foundation for your success. It takes planning, delayed gratification, and just plain old smart money sense.

Bottom line is this: be diligent about your savings, take it seriously, plan ahead and keep that vision of financial independence in the forefront of your thoughts—not the newest phone or a closet full of clothes.

How should you allocate your savings?

The allocation of your savings will depend upon your age. As you get older and have more financial obligations, more of your money will go towards your needs, such as car, mortgage/rent, utilities, food, etc.

Let's break it up into two different age groups. Ages 12–16 will have one set of allocation rules, and 16 and older will have another.

So, let's talk about 12–16 year old's to start. Since you do not have the responsibilities of a car and other expenses just yet, you are able to allocate more towards savings (for your car). You probably do not have other need requirements. Here is my recommendation for the allocation of your income. By the way, this income includes money from a job, money from gifts, such as birthday money, jobs around the house, babysitting or any other source of income.

If you are 12–16 years old, you should allocate:

30% Play money

30% Short-term savings

30% Long-term savings

10% Giving back

Play money: Thirty percent of your income can go towards just having plain ol' fun. This may be eating out with friends, buying a new gadget, going to the movies, or downloading your favorite music, etc. Whatever your little heart desires. If you have a cell phone and you have a monthly bill to pay, you can take it out of play money or short-term savings. It just depends on what you are saving for and how important that item is. Either way, you need to budget for that obligation.

Short-term savings: Thirty percent should go to short-term savings. This category would include things like a new laptop you may want, a new cell phone, maybe a new technology item, etc. Try to keep this category for things that will benefit you somehow. For example, the new laptop can help with school.

Long-term savings: Thirty percent of your money should go to long-term savings. This would include money for your car, starting your investment account, or even college. Having money as a cushion for unforeseen circumstances is a good mindset to have early in life too! You should not touch this money!

Giving back: Ten percent should go back to the world somehow. I recommend you find a charity that touches your heart and make regular contributions. You can also give back to your religious organization or a local family in need. Giving back is so important, as I will discuss in a later chapter.

If you are 16 years or older, you should allocate:

50% Needs

30% Wants (short-term savings)

10% Long-term savings

10% Giving back

Needs: This would include all your expenses relating to your car, including car payments, car insurance, car maintenance and gas. It would also include cell phone payments, rent, utilities, food, and other needs. These expenses will obviously be much different when you move out of your parents' home. Either way, 50% should go towards needs. As you become an adult and have additional obligations, your allocations should follow closely to this model.

Wants: This would include two different umbrellas. One umbrella would be play money, such as entertainment, eating out, etc. The other umbrella would be short-term savings for those same items I mentioned above. The wants category covers both play and short-term savings because you now have more financial obligations.

Long-term savings: Personally, I would like to see more than 10% of your money go to long-term savings. If you can bring your expenses down (needs), try to add to long-term savings. This money will ramp up your investment accounts, perhaps set you up for buying your first home or starting your own business. This becomes a question of your priorities. As mentioned earlier, the sooner you start saving, the sooner the compounding can start. We all like free money.

Giving back: The same 10% rule applies that I mentioned earlier. It's a wonderful feeling to help others.

Overall, I hope you realize the importance of savings. It comes down to lifestyle choices and healthy habits. As I mentioned, it's just like eating healthy. Good choices will bring good results. It is not always easy, I will give you that. And, just like dieting, it's okay to cheat once in a while. You need to have an overall healthy perspective on your finances, with a solid foundation in place.

I have seen so many situations where a person's savings account has rescued them through a tough time. Unfortunately, these challenging times can come at us fast, so you will not have time to prepare. Whether it is unforeseen medical expenses, a surprise job loss or other personal financial hits, it always helps to be prepared. Keep in mind, most of these expenses are completely unexpected, so have a cushion to fall back on.

Action Items

What does saving money require?

_____

_____

_____

_____

_____

What are two ways that you can increase your savings?

_____

_____

What are your top five priorities for your future financial independence?

_____

_____

_____

_____

_____

What motivates you to be financially independent? Is it peace of mind? Ability to give back? The freedom you will experience? Explain in detail.

_____

_____

_____

_____

_____
_____
_____
_____
_____

What are you willing to give up today in order for you to experience a much better tomorrow?

_____
_____
_____
_____
_____

Whom should you pay first and why?

_____
_____
_____
_____
_____

What's one easy step towards becoming a millionaire? What do you think will be the most difficult thing about sacrificing today for the bigger, long-term picture?

_____
_____
_____
_____
_____

We spent a lot of time with compounding interest comparisons. What did you take away from that? What excites you the most?

_____

_____

_____

_____

_____

_____

What are your actions steps from here?

_____

_____

_____

_____

_____

Have you researched a savings or mutual fund account to set up an automatic payment plan? Where and how much will you commit to?

_____

_____

_____

_____

_____

9

Investing Basics–How to Put Your Money to Work

"I have missed more than 9000 shots in my career. I have lost almost 300 games. On 26 occasions, I have been entrusted to take the game winning shot and I missed. I have failed over and over and over again in my life. And that is why I have succeeded."

Michael Jordan

Note: This chapter was reviewed by FINRA, which allows Financial Planners to share with clients and remain in compliance. Therefore, only minor changes were made to this chapter from the 1ˢᵗ edition in order to stay in compliance. It is chock full of great, timeless information!

It's very exciting to think about starting to invest. Investing is all about making the money you have, making you more money. There are many options to consider and some basics to know before taking that leap.

As with everything I have discussed in this book, it is important to do your homework and have a good understanding of what you are doing before you jump in. You will be learning many new concepts and a new vocabulary that may seem overwhelming at first. Don't let this stop you. Doing nothing could cost you money in the long run. Enjoy the learning process and do not do anything until you fully understand what you are doing.

I mentioned earlier that investing is about making the money you have make you more money. The two most popular ways to do this are investing in real estate and investing in the stock market. (As a side note, investing in yourself is on the top of this list, but not the topic of this chapter.)

This chapter is going to cover the stock market basics. Many people have made fortunes in both the real estate market and the stock market. My suggestion is that you tap into both, but only when you are ready.

Here is a quick overview of the topics I am going to cover:

Definitions of some of the vocabulary you will hear

- Type of stocks
- Type of bonds

- Mutual funds—a great consideration for you
- Cash equivalents that offer less risk
- What diversification means and why you must have it

Let me start by saying this information will be basic in nature. I want to introduce this world to you, without "fire hosing" you. There are many wonderful books that will teach you advanced techniques, such as trading options, understanding commodities, charting, and so much more. The information in this book will be a great foundation for you to get started.

If this information seems a bit hard to follow, just reread it and take in what you can. Referring back to this information is a great way to take this in, little by little.

Some definitions

I realize the basic definitions can be boring, but it helps to understand some of the vocabulary as you gain momentum here. If necessary, come back and refer to it later.

Let's start with some basic definitions:

Bear Market: A time where there is widespread pessimism in the financial markets and there has been a long period of stock prices falling. Simply put, the stock market is going down.

Bull Market: A prolonged period of time where stock prices rise faster than the historical average. (People are happy because their stock values are going up.)

Diversification: Allocating your funds into various investment types to help reduce your overall risk. Some investments will do better than others at any given time. It is a helpful strategy, but cannot ensure a profit or protect against a loss.

Dow (or DJIA): The Dow Jones Industrial Average. It the *price weighted average* of thirty significant stocks traded on the New York Stock Exchange and the NASDAQ. The Dow was invented by Charles Dow in 1896 and originally tracked only twelve stocks. The list grew to its current size of thirty stocks in 1928. It is the single most watched index in the world and includes companies like General Electric, Disney, Exxon, and Microsoft. When you hear TV networks discussing "the market being up or down," they are generally referring to the Dow.

NYSE: The New York Stock Exchange is the oldest and largest stock exchange in the United States. It still uses a large trading floor where brokers of buyers and sellers do their transactions.

NASDAQ: The National Association of Securities Dealers Automated Quotation System. This is a computerized system that facilitates the trading of stocks. Unlike the NYSE, the NASDAQ does not have a physical trading place that brings actual buyers and sellers together. It was created in 1971 and provides price quotations for over 5,000 actively traded stocks. The NASDAQ is traditionally home to many high tech stocks, such as Intel and Dell.

S&P 500: The Standard and Poor's index of 500 stocks chosen for market size, liquidity and industry grouping, among other factors. The S&P 500 is one of the most commonly used benchmarks for the overall U.S. stock market. The Dow was at one time the most renowned index for U.S. stocks, but because it contains only thirty companies, most people agree that the S&P 500 is a better representation of the U.S. market. In fact, many consider it to be the definition of the market.

Earnings per share: The total earnings of a company divided by their number of shares outstanding.

Inflation: The term used to represent a rise in prices. Inflation usually occurs when there is too much money in circulation and not enough goods and services. Prices will rise when there is this excess demand.

Recession: A significant decline in activity across the economy, typically lasting 6–18 months. The technical indicator of a recession is two consecutive quarters of negative economic growth as measured by a country's gross domestic product (GDP). Recession is a normal, although unpleasant, part of the business cycle.

Money market fund: This is a mutual fund that invests in short term debt. The money is very liquid (which means you can get it anytime) and is considered a cash equivalent.

It usually offers a better rate than your bank checking and savings accounts.

Mutual fund: An investment vehicle that is made up of a pool of funds collected from many investors for the purpose of investing in securities such as stocks, bonds, money market instruments, and similar assets. Mutual funds are operated by money managers, who invest the fund's capital and attempt to produce capital gains and income for the fund's investors. One of the main advantages of mutual funds is that they give small investors access to professionally managed, diversified portfolios of equities, bonds, and other securities, which would be quite difficult (if not impossible) to create with a small amount of capital. This is a popular way to start investing in the stock market.

Stock: A holder of stock (a shareholder) has a claim to a part of the corporation's assets and earnings. In other words, a shareholder is an owner of a company. Ownership is determined by the number of shares a person owns relative to the number of outstanding shares. For example, if a company has 1,000 shares of stock outstanding and one person owns 100 shares, that person would own and have claim to 10% of the company's assets. There are two main types of stock: common and preferred. Common stock usually entitles the owner to vote at shareholders' meetings and to receive dividends. Preferred stock generally does not have voting rights, but has a higher claim on assets and earnings than the common shares. For example, owners of preferred stock receive dividends before common shareholders and have priority in the event that a company goes bankrupt and is liquidated.

There are many more definitions that pertain to the financial markets, but these are some key ones with which to start. There is also a great website for more advanced definitions and market information: www.investopedia.com.

So, let's talk stocks

As mentioned in the definition section, a stock is part ownership of a company. If the company does well and has good earnings and growth, the stock value (price) will generally go up. If the opposite happens and the company does poorly, the value goes down. The trick, of course, is to know which one of the thousands of stocks to purchase.

Over the long term, stocks have historically outperformed all other investment classes. From 1926 to 2006, the S&P 500 returned an average annual 10.4% gain.

On the flip side, do not invest in stocks if you need the money in the short term. Over the short term, stocks fluctuate based on everything from interest rates to gas prices to the latest hurricane. If you need the money to purchase something in less than 3–5 years, I do not recommend buying stock. It would be a total bummer if it were time to buy a car or your first home, only to find your money worth less than when you started.

When it comes time to invest in the stock market, I am going to recommend you start with a mutual fund. A mutual fund allows you to diversify into different sectors (businesses that have different products and services). In other words, you will spread out your risk if you have your money in different companies, within different arenas. I will cover more on mutual funds shortly, but for now, just know that when you get started, consider mutual funds over a single company stock.

So, how do you decide which stock? This is where your research and due diligence comes in. By the way, do not buy a stock on a recommendation from a friend. Although friends always mean well, make sure to research the stock yourself or work with a Certified Financial Planner.

This can be a bit advanced, so take it slow and refer back to it often. For fun, you can watch a company that offers a product you enjoy. If you love Nike shoes, watch Nike. If you love Coke, watch Coca Cola.

To get an idea, you can "paper trade" stocks before you put your real money in the trade. Paper trading means that you "buy" a stock with pretend money. I will call it your monopoly money. You do not actually buy the stock with real funds, you just pretend you bought at a certain price and time, based on your homework, and then sold it when you thought it was a good time. You then track your profit or losses. This is a great way to get your feet wet and gain confidence at the same time. There are several websites that allow you to set up an account for free to paper trade.

So, how do you analyze a stock? There are two popular ways that companies are analyzed.

Fundamental analysis means analyzing a stock based on earnings, revenues, future growth, return on equity, profit margins, and other data to determine a company's underlying value and potential for future growth. With fundamental analysis, you are trying to determine a company's intrinsic value as well. (Intrinsic value is the value given to a company based on underlying *perception of value*. McDonald's would be an example of a company with intrinsic value.) You are looking at their books to determine if the company is strong, with a favorable future.

Technical analysis does not try to determine intrinsic value; rather the analysis is focused on market activity, such as past prices and volume. Technical analysts use charts and other tools to identify patterns that may suggest future activity.

Although this piece of information is a bit advanced, I wanted you to be aware that these categories exist. Stocks can be broken down into different categories including: large cap, mid-cap, small cap and International. "Cap" is short for capitalization, which is the total stock market value of all the shares of a company's stock. This is calculated by multiplying the stock price by the number of shares outstanding.

Generally speaking, large cap stock refers to companies with a market capitalization of greater than $5 billion, while small cap refers to companies with a market capitalization of less than $3 billion. Mid-cap are those that fall between the two. International is a non-U.S. company.

On to the bonds

Bonds are like an IOU. You get to lend a borrower some money, and they in return promise to pay you back that money, plus interest. A specific date (maturity date) and interest rate (the coupon rate) are in place as well.

The main categories of bonds are corporate bonds, municipal bonds, and governmental bonds. U.S. treasury bonds (governmental) are referred to as notes, bills, or bonds, depending upon their maturity duration. If you hear the term "treasuries," it is referring to the governmental bonds, notes, and bills.

A treasury bill (also called T-bill) has a maturity of less than one year, a treasury note has a maturity between one and ten years, and a bond has a maturity greater than ten years.

Here's an example: If you were to buy a $1,000 bond, with a coupon rate of 4% simple interest, payable in two years, you would get $20 interest paid semi-annually, or $40 per year. That means you would be paid twice per year. At the end of the two years, you would receive your $1,000 principal back.

With a treasury bill (maturity less than one year), you will not receive interest semi-annually. You would actually buy the bill at a *discount* and receive the face value of the bill at maturity. The discounted amount would depend on the interest rate and duration to maturity.

Government bonds are considered relatively safe. Even though U.S. government bonds are backed by the full faith and credit of the U.S. government, the bonds are subject to share price fluctuations and if sold before maturity, are subject to loss of principal. There is risk, which is why it is important to do your homework. Many bonds are rated by agencies, such as Moody's and Standard and Poor's. These agencies grade the financial standing of the issuer to help you make better decisions.

Like most investments in the financial markets, there is a risk vs. reward payoff. The higher risk issuer (generally graded lower) will offer higher returns (higher interest rates.) In general, the bond market is volatile, and fixed income securities carry interest rate risk. This means that as interest rates rise, bond prices usually fall, and vice versa. This effect is usually more pronounced for longer-term securities. An investor may also lose principal if a bond is not held until maturity. You will need to decide your risk tolerance and length of time you have to invest to determine which bond makes sense.

Again, when you are starting out, I would recommend you look into mutual funds. These are a great way to stay diversified, while investing in bonds of different types.

One more thing about bonds: depending upon the type of bond in which you invest, there can be some tax benefits involved. It is beyond the scope of this book to discuss the tax advantages, but just know that when you decide to invest in bonds, be sure to explore the tax consequences.

Mutual funds

As I have mentioned earlier, mutual funds are a popular way to get started in the financial markets. They are very simple to invest in, easily liquidated (meaning you can get your money out quickly) and allows for easy diversification. There are many different types of funds from which to choose, and asking yourself three basic questions will help you decide which makes the most sense for you.

First, ask yourself, "What is my goal?" Are you looking for more income or safety?

Second, "What is my time frame?" Will you need this money in the next few months or is this investment for longer-term needs? As mentioned, I would not recommend the stock market if you need the money in three years or less. You are better off putting those funds into a money market account.

Third, "how much risk am I willing to take?" Generally speaking, the riskier the investment, the higher return potential. If you aren't comfortable with the riskier investments, understand your return may not be as good. This is a very personal decision, and either way is completely acceptable.

If you have a longer time horizon, such as five years or more, you may be able to afford to go with a bit riskier mutual fund. You must have the stomach to ride the ups and downs of the market, but over the long run, stocks generally do well.

So, what are your choices?

Here is the list of various types of mutual funds.

Money Market Funds: These funds generally invest in short term U.S. treasury bills, certificate of deposits (CDs) or commercial paper. Although they are not FDIC insured, they are considered relatively safe investments. These will tend to have better returns than savings accounts, but because they are considered lower risk investments, the returns will not be anything exciting. Sometimes boring is good, especially if you will need the money in the near future.

Bond Funds: These funds are a pool of bonds, typically invested in corporate, municipal or government bonds. Just as the bonds described earlier, they are typically more conservative than a stock. Bond funds fall between the money market fund and stock funds when discussing risk and reward. They are less risky than stock funds, but riskier than money market funds. As a result, you will typically receive a higher return in a bond fund than you would a money market fund, but less than a stock fund.

Stock funds: There is a huge choice of stock funds, with various risk levels associated with them. Some funds' primary goal is income, while others are more growth focused. Deciding which one makes the most sense for you will depend on how you answered those previous three questions. It is important to understand that as the market goes up or down, the value of your investment will go up and down. There is no guarantee that you will not lose money. In fact, you will see your account fluctuate day to day, but remember, when you invest in the stock market, you should be investing for the long term. By long term, I mean at least four to five years.

Hybrid funds: This type of fund invests in both stocks and bonds. They are also called balanced funds, blended funds, or asset allocation funds. These funds have the goal of both investment growth and stability. I personally like this type of fund, as it diversifies for me.

Some final thoughts on mutual funds

When shopping for a mutual fund, make sure you do your homework. I realize I have said this several times, but it is that important. Research the past performance, and watch for fees. Although past performance will never guarantee any future results, it is always good to compare to other funds. I recommend a no-load (which means no commissions) fund. You can research all this information very easily online.

ETF's

Another, relatively new product to consider, is an Exchange Traded Fund.

"In the simplest terms, Exchange Traded Funds (ETFs) are funds that track indexes like the NASDAQ-100 Index, S&P 500, Dow Jones, etc. When you buy shares of an ETF, you are buying shares of a portfolio that tracks the yield and return of its native index. The main difference between ETFs and other types of index funds is that ETFs don't try to outperform their corresponding index, but simply replicate its performance.

ETFs have been around since the early 1980s, but they've come into their own within the past 10 years. ETFs combine the range of a diversified portfolio with the simplicity of trading a single stock.

ETF shares trade exactly like stocks. Unlike index mutual funds, which are priced only after market closings, ETFs are priced and traded continuously throughout the trading day.

Because their value is based on an underlying index, ETFs enjoy the additional benefits of broader diversification than shares in single companies, as well as what many investors perceive as the greater flexibility that goes with investing in entire markets, sectors, regions, or asset types. Because they represent baskets of stocks, ETFs, or at least the ones based on major indexes, typically trade at much higher volumes than individual stocks. High trading volumes mean high liquidity, enabling investors to get into and out of investment positions with minimum risk and expense."[2]

Cash equivalents

Examples of these investments include checking accounts, savings accounts, money market accounts, CDs, and T-bills. CDs (certificate of deposits) can be shorter term, such as three months, or longer term, sometimes five years. This investment type falls into the category of lower risk, lower return. If you need your money in the short term or for emergency money, this is a great place to stash the cash.

Diversify, diversify, diversify

After reading through the various types of investment options, I hope you see the importance of being diversified. The market can be very volatile and putting all your eggs in one basket can be a costly mistake. Having your funds in various growth, income, bond and money market accounts is important. Typically, when one aspect of the market is doing well, the other is not, and vice versa.

Once you decide which fund(s) you like, consider what is called "dollar cost averaging." Let me explain. Rather than investing all your money at one time into a fund, consider buying into that fund in increments. This will *average out* the cost of that investment.

---

[2] www.nasdaq.com

For example, if you had $2,000 to invest, consider buying into the fund in $500 increments over four consecutive months. This allows for buying more shares when the price is lower. This also lessens the risk of investing a larger amount at the wrong time. Plus, an added benefit is you will get into the habit of investing on a regular monthly basis. You need to consider your ability to invest during these fluctuations. Neither diversification nor dollar cost averaging can ensure a profit or protect against a loss.

I haven't even touched on the other markets, namely commodities, oil and gas, precious metals, real estate investment trusts, or international funds. This information is much more advanced and not necessary to get yourself started in the markets. Take it slow, do what makes you comfortable and confident, and continue to learn!

I have given you enough information to get your feet wet and start exploring. Have fun with it, but take it seriously. This is your hard-earned money we are talking about!

Action Items

How much money can you set aside every month to invest?

_____

What type of investment are you interested in exploring? Stocks? Bonds? Mutual Funds? ETFs?

Why?

_____
_____
_____
_____
_____

How do mutual funds and ETFs differ?

_____
_____
_____
_____
_____

What investment type typically carries the least amount of risk?

_____

What investment type typically carries the most amount of risk?

_____

Explain why diversification is a good investment strategy.

_____

_____

_____

_____

_____

What is dollar cost averaging and why is this strategy beneficial?

_____

_____

_____

Contact two mutual fund companies, such as Vanguard or Fidelity Investments, and speak to a representative. Ask them how you can get started and explore the various funds. The representative can help you determine which funds make the most sense, given your investment goals and risk tolerance. Explain what this conversation taught you.

_____

_____

_____

_____

_____

_____

_____

10

Buying your First Home!

"Success is stumbling from failure to failure
with no loss of enthusiasm."
Winston Churchill

Note for parents: This information is geared toward the young adult. Younger kids will benefit from this, but the older (20+) child will better relate, as they may be thinking about buying a home in the near future. The following information is a bit more technical and advanced; however, it is a wonderful reference tool for later. I would recommend reading this now, but referring back to this when actually buying a home as well.

Although you may not be looking at buying a home anytime soon, this is invaluable information to know early on. Some of this information can be a bit overwhelming, but if you read it slowly and fully understand it, you will reap priceless rewards. I do admit, it can be a bit dry at times, but please stick with me on this. Reread it as often as needed and use as a reference tool for later.

Buying your first new home is one of the most exciting things you will experience. Having independence and a place to call your own will bring you such a feeling of freedom and empowerment.

Where do you start when it is time to buy your first place? There are many different elements that go into buying a home, but when broken down into separate subjects, they become easy to handle. Here are the key elements that we will discuss:

1)   Credit scores

2)   Down payment

3)   Closing costs

4)   Loan types

5)   Where to buy

Credit scores

I covered credit scores at great length in another chapter, but let me emphasize how important a good credit score is to your mortgage payment. Without a good score (at the time of this writing, a good score would be 720 or above), your interest rate will be higher, costing you thousands of dollars over time.

The lenders (banks who would lend you money) are going to charge you a higher interest rate if they feel you are a higher risk borrower. The credit score tells them how well you have been able to manage your credit, which in turn, gives them an indication of how much risk you are to them. Higher risk equals higher rate. Lower risk equals lower rate. That goes for everything you purchase on credit. We covered this at length in the credit chapter.

Let's use an example that may be easier to understand. These numbers are for instructional purposes only and do not represent today's rates.

Let's say you buy a home and your mortgage is $250,000. A thirty-year fixed, fully amortized mortgage (fully amortized simply means you are paying principal and interest in your monthly mortgage payment) with a 720 score may have an interest rate of 6.50%. Your mortgage payment only (not including property taxes and insurance) would be $1,580.17.

Now, let's say your credit score is less than perfect, so the lender charges you 7.25%. Seems like no big deal, but check out this math. Now your payment goes to $1,705.44, a difference of $125.27 per month. That is $1,503.25 a year. That is almost enough to pay an entire month's mortgage payment. If you stay in the house for five years, or do not refinance out of that loan, that costs you $7,516.24 for that five-year period—even more if you stay in longer. I cannot emphasize enough how imperative it is to get your credit scores up and keep them up.

Down payment

The down payment represents the amount of money you plan to put towards your home purchase. Much like a "deposit." It is also referred to as your "'equity."

Let me digress here one minute regarding your equity. As real estate values go up and down, your equity value will increase or decrease. The wonderful thing about real estate is that over time, typically, values will increase and you will enjoy an increased equity position, even though you did not put more money down. That is why real estate is a wonderful addition to a balanced, diversified investment portfolio. Real estate, much like investing in the stock market, should be considered a long-term investment.

Side note: Some real estate investors will "flip" homes, meaning they purchase a home, which oftentimes needs repair or updating. They make the repairs and updates, then turn around and sell for a profit, usually in a short time period. I will not expand on this topic, but wanted you to know there are different strategies when investing in real estate.

To get the most attractive rate on your loan, you will need at least a 20% down payment. For example, if you buy a home for $300,000, a 20% down payment would equal $60,000, resulting in a loan amount of $240,000. If you are thinking, "Where am I going to get *that* kind of money?" Don't worry, there are other options.

There are loans available that require less than 20% down, that have competitive interest rates, assuming, yes, you have good credit.

As of this writing, conventional financing allows for 5% down payment, for loan amounts of $417,000 or less. If your loan is greater than $417,000, but less than $625,500, you will need 10% down payment. There are additional loan programs, but these are the basic.

FHA is a great alternative requiring only 3½% down payment (as of this writing) and allows for gift funds, seller-paid closing costs, and less than perfect credit scores. FHA stands for Federal Housing Administration, which is a governmental agency that insures mortgages. "Seller paid closing costs," means that the seller of the home is allowed to pay for some of *your* closing costs, such as title, escrow, appraisal, and more. We will touch more on that in a bit. It helps you get into the home with less of your cash out of pocket.

Anytime you put less than 20% down on a home, you are required to pay PMI, which stands for *private mortgage insurance*. In simple terms, it is an insurance policy to protect lenders in case a borrower defaults (stops making his mortgage payments). You have to pay the insurance premium, which adds to your monthly payment. With FHA loans, you will have this monthly insurance premium, and an upfront insurance cost.

There is no secret science to having a nice down payment—spend less and save more. If you start saving early and invest it wisely, you will have a nice down payment before you know it. Watch the spending habits, as discussed earlier, and you will be in your own home sooner than you think.

Closing costs

Closing costs are those costs that you have to pay when you buy or refinance a home. There are many people and fingers involved, and everybody gets paid, one way or another. Closing costs can be broken down into two different categories: non-recurring and recurring. You will also have a possible third category: impounds.

Let's start with **non-recurring**. Just as the name implies these are costs that *do not reoccur* each month. They are one-time costs associated with the purchase or refinance. Examples of these costs are title insurance, escrow (what we use in California, some states use attorneys), appraisal, underwriting (the person who works for the lender and reviews your loan—they give you the thumbs up or thumbs down), processing, recording fees, notary fees, and other small miscellaneous costs.

In addition, you will have the option to pay a *loan origination* or *loan discount fee*. This is also referred to as paying *points*. By paying a loan origination or discount fee (point), you are buying your interest rate down on your mortgage. One point equals one percent of your loan amount. Two points equals two percent of your loan amount. I would not recommend you ever pay more than one point. Always calculate the breakeven point to determine if it makes sense to pay the one point. Make sure you seek the advice of a mortgage specialist you trust.

I know this can be a bit confusing so let's use an example:

Let's say your loan amount equals $200,000 (whether you buy or refinance, the same rules apply). If you decide to pay one point, that would cost you $2,000, which is *in addition* to your other nonrecurring closing costs. Let's say your rate would be 6.00% with one point, but if you chose zero points, your rate would be 6.25%. (This is typically, but not always the difference in rate, about 0.25 %.)

Your payment on a $200,000 mortgage at 6.00% would be $1,199.10 (fixed rate, principal and interest). Your payment at 6.25% would be $1,231.43, resulting in a difference of $32.33 per month. To determine if it makes sense to pay the point or not, we would divide the $2,000/32.33 to see how many months it would take before we broke even. In this example, it would take 61.86 months, or just over five years.

What this means is that if we paid the $2,000 upfront, we would not benefit from that expense until five years from now. In this case, I would not recommend you pay the point; it is too long before you get your money back. You will probably move or refinance that loan before that five-year term, so it does not make much sense. I like to see three years or less for a breakeven point before I recommend paying a point. Cash is king, especially when buying your first home, so paying that additional point is not the best idea. Having said all that, if the seller is willing to pay some closing costs, including a point, this can be a great way to buy your rate down.

Recurring costs are those that reoccur every month: interest payments, homeowner's insurance, and property taxes and where applicable, homeowner's association dues. Depending upon what day of the month you close escrow, you will have prorated interest to pay.

You will owe interest to the new lender for a portion of the month that you own the home. For example, if you close escrow on the tenth of the month, you will owe twenty days of interest to the lender (assuming a thirty-day month). This twenty days of interest is part of your closing costs that you need to pay at close of escrow.

Here's an interesting little side note. When you make your mortgage payment on the first of the month, you are actually paying for the *prior* month. For example, when you pay your mortgage on June 1, you are actually paying the interest for May. The technical term is "arrears." (By the way, your payment is due on the first of the month, considered late on the fifteenth. Don't be late. Being late on a mortgage payment will hurt your credit score terribly and may impact your ability to obtain a mortgage for one year.)

Back to recurring costs—you will have the prorated interest we discussed, and you will have prorated property taxes, which essentially follows the same process as interest. Depending upon when you close escrow, you will owe property taxes from that date. Now, this gets a bit tricky.

In California, for example, property taxes are paid twice per year. When we pay those taxes, we pay for six-month increments. In California, the first installment is due November 1 and is considered delinquent if not paid by December 10. The second installment is due February 1, delinquent April 10. It is beyond the scope of this book to explain how the property taxes work, but know that you will owe a prorated portion at the close of escrow.

Make sure you do your homework and get an approximate amount due so you have a full understanding of your closing costs. Lenders are required to give you a loan estimate at the beginning of your mortgage process, which will break these numbers down for you. (Formerly known as a good faith estimate)

A one-year homeowner's insurance premium will also be due at time of closing. Contact an insurance agent that you trust, or are referred to, to obtain a quote on a homeowner's policy.

Impounds, also known as escrow accounts, and are required when you put less than a 10% down payment, as of this writing. They are optional if you put 10% or more down. An impound account is an account that the lender has set aside for you, much like a saving account in your name, that accumulates your property taxes and homeowners insurance on a monthly basis.

Every month you pay your normal mortgage payment, you would also include the monthly portion of taxes and insurance. This budgets that money for you. When those large expenses come due, the lender then pays that out of your impound account.

Some people prefer an impound account because if forces them to save for those expenses monthly. Others prefer to save themselves and enjoy the interest on the money they are saving. It really becomes a personal choice.

If you are disciplined enough to save monthly, I would recommend you do not have the lender impound and you enjoy the interest on your own money while it sits in your savings account. I suggest having an automatic withdrawal set up with your checking account and a separate savings account for this expense. Having the money taken out automatically does not give you the choice to forget. Having said that, some lenders and states may require you to impound, so be sure to check beforehand.

I realize this is a lot of information to take in. I also realize it can be a bit boring. Just refer back to it as needed. It is imperative you understand how this works. It can save you a lot of money and headache in the long run.

Once you are in the market to purchase a home, this information will make a lot more sense to you! You will also appreciate it more.

Loan types

Although there are some unique loan programs today, here are the more common loan types you will find. I am going to cover only these loan types, as other programs may, or may not be, available at a later date.

- 30 year fixed, fully amortized
- ARMs (adjustable rate mortgage)
- FHA

For the most part, sticking with the simple, vanilla type loan is best, if you plan to stay in the home more than 5-7 years. By simple vanilla, I mean a thirty-year fixed, fully amortized loan. This means that your rate is locked for thirty years, or the life of the loan, and pays down the principal and interest. It is simple, it is conservative and it is safe.

There are no surprises with interest rate fluctuations, and you are paying off your mortgage over time. There are also fifteen- and twenty-year, fixed, fully amortized loans.

The payments on these would be higher than the thirty-year because the loan is being amortized, or paid off, a lot quicker. Typically, though, the interest rates on these loans are lower than the thirty-year fixed.

Be careful with the fifteen- or twenty-year loan, only because you are locked into that higher payment. If you ever have a financial issue arise, you must come up with the higher monthly payment when you may not be able to afford it. This is just something to think about when deciding which loan program to go with. With the fifteen or twenty-year loan, your equity is growing faster, which is certainly a nice benefit.

ARM's, or adjustable rate mortgages, are an alternative that may make sense for some. ARMs come in several forms: three year, five year, seven year and ten year are the most common. These loans offer fixed rates for the first 3/5/7/10 years, then the loan becomes adjustable, meaning the rate will fluctuate after that. I only recommend this type of loan if you know, for certain, that you will be out of this loan before the loan adjusts. This works well for those who plan to move, or know they will be refinancing in the next few years.

These loans typically have a lower interest rate, which is why people are attracted to them. If you end up staying with the loan for some reason, when your payment adjusts you may experience payment shock. This is how many people get in trouble. If you are considering this type of loan, be sure that you are out before the rate adjusts.

FHA

I touched on this loan type earlier. It is a very popular loan, especially with first time homebuyers. It requires the lowest down payment, the underwriting guidelines are more lenient and allows for higher debt to income ratios.

Make sure to discuss all your loan options with a reputable loan advisor, preferably one that is referred to you. A good mortgage advisor will ask you questions about your intentions, future financial plans and really understand your current situation. Better yet, call me! I would love to help you get into your home!

Side note: I have created short videos, specifically for first time homebuyers, which can be found on my website at www.PattiHandy.com. Click on the 'home buying coach' link and enjoy!

Where to buy

In the real estate world, you will hear, "location, location, location" and for good reason. The specific location, even within the same city, can make a difference in your home's appreciation over time. Do your homework, talk to local people, talk to several agents and take your time investigating. This will probably be the largest financial investment you make, so do not rush through it.

From a purely investment perspective, find a location that has experienced strong real estate appreciation, has had strong growth in the work force, a climate that you enjoy, a low crime rate, and excellent school districts, just to name a few.

Sometimes just driving around a neighborhood, getting a sense of what people are doing to their homes, will give you an idea of the pride of ownership within the area. Take your time and enjoy the journey of searching.

Some states are more affordable than others are, and it is best to find a home that feels right for you. I can tell you from personal experience that being near your family is a wonderful gift. The quality of your life is enhanced with your family and friends surrounding you, so hopefully you can find a home close by.

Some final thoughts

It is beyond the scope of this book to go into the calculations that lenders use to approve you for a loan. They will look at your expenses relative to your income and use certain ratios to give you a yes or no vote.

Beware, they may approve you for a loan that *may not feel comfortable for you*. If you are told that you can afford a $300,000 home, based on your ratios, but after doing the math, you are comfortable with the monthly payment on a $250,000 home, by all means follow your gut. Don't let someone talk you into a loan or home because it will earn them a bigger commission.

Also, make sure you have at least six months of living expenses tucked away in a savings account. This should include mortgage payment, property taxes, and homeowners insurance. Keep the money in a liquid account, such as a money market account, just in case you need it quickly. Ignore the temptation to tap into this money for furniture or other goodies for your new place. Put the money aside and forget you have it.

Your new home will bring you so much joy as you make it your own. Sharing it with those you love will make for some serious fun and wonderful memories.

Action Items

List the five major components to consider when buying a home.

_____

_____

_____

_____

_____

Why is it important to pull your credit score early, well before you plan to buy a home?

_____

_____

_____

_____

_____

Why is it important that you do not make any major purchases before you buy a home?

_____

_____

_____

_____

_____

Define the term, down payment? What is it also referred to?

_____

_____

_____

_____

_____

What percentage of down payment do you need for the best interest rate?

_____

What does FHA stand for?

_____

List some advantages to the FHA loan.

_____

_____

_____

_____

_____

What does PMI stand for?

_____

_____

_____

_____

_____

When and why would you have private mortgage insurance?

_____

_____

_____

_____

_____

Name the three categories of closing costs.

_____

_____

_____

Give an example of a recurring closing cost.

_____

_____

_____

_____

_____

How is 'one point' calculated on your closing costs? How much is a point on a $300,000 loan amount?

_____

_____

_____

_____

_____

When does it make sense to pay points?

_____

_____
_____
_____

What are the advantages and disadvantages of having an impound (escrow) account?

_____
_____
_____
_____
_____
_____
_____
_____

Describe the advantages and disadvantages of an adjustable rate mortgage (ARM)?

_____
_____
_____
_____
_____

List some of the most important factors to consider when buying a home.

_____
_____
_____
_____

What are some of the questions you have regarding mortgages and buying your first home?

_____

_____

_____

_____

_____

11

Giving Back is the Greatest Gift of All

*"The best way to find yourself is to
lose yourself in the service of others."*
Mahatma Gandhi

I have purposely left this chapter as the last one in the book. Not because it is the least important—no, actually quite the opposite. It is so important that I wanted this to be the last section you read, which will hopefully be on the forefront of your mind.

All this wealth knowledge, money skills and financial wisdom is not for accumulating *things*. It is not meant to teach you how to afford the fanciest car, biggest house, or latest gadget. This isn't just about material wealth, but also about spiritual and emotional wealth.

Having a nice home and car is wonderful, but not at the expense of your financial freedom. By *my* definition, financial freedom is not only having the funds available to take care of you and your family, but also share it with the world and give back to society.

Side note for parents: Your kids are watching you! Nothing encourages your kids more than to see you do the same. Consider matching the donation dollar for dollar, which supports both the organization and your child. Work as a family to volunteer your time and decide where to allocate your family's contributions.

Don't get me wrong. I want you to enjoy the finer things in life. My desire is for you to live in a home that feels like your sanctuary away from the world, be able to afford dining out whenever you want, wear the clothes that please you, travel if you wish, and simply enjoy life to its fullest. It's a delicate balancing act, as I do not want you focused on *things*. Those things will never bring you true happiness, at least not for long.

Oftentimes, we spend money to fill an emotional void. Please try to avoid this and be aware of why you want something. Buying on a bad day or emotional whim will only create more stress for you when the bill arrives later. Enjoy your life and treat yourself to gifts that feed your soul, not the neighbors' impression of you.

Giving away money is not the only thing I want you giving away. I want you to share *you* with the world. Devote your time and skills to a cause that resonates with you. Take the time necessary to find your *purpose in life*. That is a question that so many people struggle with, but when the answer is revealed, it can be life changing. You have so many gifts and talents to share, please embrace those and let them shine for everyone to see. Take your time and enjoy the journey to find that purpose. Be patient and know that it will be revealed at the right time. You need to be looking for it. Seek it. Ask for it. Then be still.

As I write this, there are some major shifts happening in our world, including our workforce. Gone are the days of stability and working for corporate America. Benefits, hours, and more are being taken away, bit by bit. As a result, many are looking at alternatives, namely being self-employed.

Whether you work for someone else or take the entrepreneurial route, please be in a place of *purposeful service*. Find a way to make a difference in the world, find a way to give back, find a way to improve the lives of others. This will bring you more joy than the latest gadget, while feeding your soul with inner happiness.

In order to find the right path for yourself, I encourage you to take some quiet time and think about this: What are some of your *talents*? What are your shining *skills*? What do you *love* to do? How can you use this in a way that will generate cash for you *and* serve the world? Think about creating a business that utilizes your talents and skills that you also enjoy. Look for a business model or business plan that works for you. I discussed some of this in another chapter, but I want to bring this back to focus.

You do not necessarily need to create a business model from scratch. Find one that works successfully, that is aligned with your value system. Allow your creativity to soar, and just think to yourself, "If I knew I couldn't fail, what would I want to do?"

There are no limits for you. You are an amazing person and can do anything you set your mind to. You just have to want it bad enough. You have to have a plan, define your dream, set your goals, and do not listen to any negative noise that you may hear. Surround yourself with positive people who believe in you and support you.

Know that you are here for a reason, for a purpose. Review the chapter on your mindset towards money and work to master that aspect. How you look at money, respect money, and understanding your beliefs toward money will be vital towards the management of your money.

I have always said that dying with millions in the bank is a tragedy. Your money needs to be shared. It needs to be given to our world and to other people. Find something: a cause, your religious organization, a health organization, or a local family.

I pray this book has brought you knowledge and skills that will help you on the road as you begin your journey. As a parent myself, my deepest desire is for my son to be healthy, happy and safe. I also want him, and you, prepared to stand on your own two feet, so that you will experience independence and confidence. The money skills taught in this book will be instrumental as you venture out. Enjoy your journey, never give up, always share your wealth and show kindness. This will bring you a full and joyful life.

"Only a life lived for others is a life worthwhile."
Albert Einstein

Action Items

List 3-5 organizations that you would like to donate to, either your time or money.

_____

_____

_____

_____

_____

How much money can you dedicate every month to give back?

_____

Considering your school and work obligations, how much time can you dedicate a week to volunteer?

_____

What was your favorite topic to learn about in this book? Why?

_____

_____

_____

_____

_____

How will the information in this book improve the quality of your life?

_____

_____

_____

_____

_____

About the Author

Patti Handy is a leading mortgage professional and expert in the California market. Patti's expertise in mortgage finance comes from over 30 years working with banks and mortgage banking firms, large and small.

What makes Patti successful, and in such high demand as a mortgage professional, are the results she achieves for her clients. Patti's passion to see her clients purchase the home of their dreams, or simply refinance existing homeowners into affordable mortgage payments, is what motivates her every single day.

Patti's commitment to helping clients make smart financial decisions came from her own life experiences. The same financial solutions and strategies that Patti used to turn her life around after her divorce are the one's she shares with her clients, so they too can enjoy the rewards of homeownership, while maintaining financial balance.

Beyond Patti's expertise in helping clients find the best possible mortgage financing for their particular needs, Patti offers something else that goes far beyond what any other mortgage professional can provide…financial education to young adults.

She was blessed with parents that taught her money smarts at a very early age, which has been an invaluable gift of knowledge. Unfortunately, our local and national education systems do not provide education regarding financial responsibility. It is for this reason that Patti created and founded **<u>Teens Cash Coach</u>**™.

Patti's commitment to educating high school and college age individuals about financial responsibility was and remains so strong that she authored a popular book, ***"How to Ditch Your Allowance and be Richer than Your Parents"*** and created an online *Money School* program.

Patti is very active in her community on many levels, as her core belief is to always give back. She is a single mom to an amazing son, who inspires her every day. She considers the beach to be her happy place, chocolate as her favorite food group, and her family and friends to be her greatest blessing.

Got questions for Patti?

Go to www.teenscashcoach.com and sign up for the four free weeks of the Online Money School Video series and receive her newsletter!

Email her directly at:

Patti@teenscashcoach.com

Bring Patti to you with *The Money School*, a fun, Online Video Money School program and workbook, which covers the information in this book and much, much more!

Visit www.teenscashcoach.com and click on "Money School" to learn more.

Remember the Free Bonus!

Email Patti to receive the "action item" worksheets you find in this book!

A great way to use over and over!

My gift to you!

Notes and Action Steps

_____

_____

_____

_____

_____

_____

_____

_____

_____

_____

_____

_____

_____

_____

_____

_____

_____

_____

_____

_____

Notes and Action Steps

_____

_____

_____

_____

_____

_____

_____

_____

_____

_____

_____

_____

_____

_____

_____

_____

_____

_____

_____

Notes and Action Steps

_____

_____

_____

_____

_____

_____

_____

_____

_____

_____

_____

_____

_____

_____

_____

_____

_____

_____

_____

_____

_____

Notes and Action Steps

Notes and Action Steps

_____

_____

_____

_____

_____

_____

_____

_____

_____

_____

_____

_____

_____

_____

_____

_____

_____

_____

_____

_____

Notes and Action Steps

Notes and Action Steps

_____

_____

_____

_____

_____

_____

_____

_____

_____

_____

_____

_____

_____

_____

_____

_____

_____

_____

_____

_____

Notes and Action Steps

_____

_____

_____

_____

_____

_____

_____

_____

_____

_____

_____

_____

_____

_____

_____

_____

_____

_____

Notes and Action Steps

_____

_____

_____

_____

_____

_____

_____

_____

_____

_____

_____

_____

_____

_____

_____

_____

_____

_____

_____

_____